CONSIDERATIONS

ON THE

DANGER AND IMPOLICY

OF

LAYING OPEN THE TRADE WITH

INDIA AND CHINA

CONSIDERATIONS

ON THE

DANGER AND IMPOLICY

OF

LAYING OPEN THE TRADE WITH

INDIA AND CHINA;

INCLUDING

AN EXAMINATION OF THE OBJECTIONS
COMMONLY URGED AGAINST

THE EAST INDIA COMPANY'S

COMMERCIAL AND FINANCIAL MANAGEMENT.

GYAN

Published by

Gyan Publishing House
5, Ansari Road
Daryaganj, New Delhi-110002
Phone: 011-47034999, 9811692060
E-mail: books@gyanbooks.com

Distribution Network
gyanbooks.com
India, USA, Canada, UK, Australia, France

ISBN: 978-81-212-9326-6 (PB)
First Published, 1812

2nd Impression 2023

Printed at: Gyan Press, Delhi.

CONSIDERATIONS ON THE DANGER AND IMPOLICY OF LAYING OPEN THE TRADE WITH INDIA AND CHINA

CONSIDERATIONS

ON THE

DANGER AND IMPOLICY

OF

LAYING OPEN THE TRADE WITH

INDIA AND CHINA;

INCLUDING

AN EXAMINATION OF THE OBJECTIONS COMMONLY URGED AGAINST THE

EAST INDIA COMPANY'S

COMMERCIAL AND FINANCIAL MANAGEMENT.

" The pretended rights of these theorists are all extremes, and in proportion
" as they are metaphysically true they are morally and politically false."

BURKE.

" Si plures sunt ii quibus improbe datum est, quam illi quibus injustum
" ademptum est, idcirco plus etiam valent?" CIC. OFF.

LONDON:

PRINTED FOR LONGMAN, HURST, REES, ORME, AND BROWN,
PATERNOSTER ROW.

1812.

THE following Sheets contain the substance of a series of Letters which appeared in the *Morning Chronicle* in the course of last summer, under the signature of COSSIM. The author finding the subject too extensive to be fully discussed within the limits of a newspaper, resolved to submit his thoughts to the Public in their present shape.

London, December, 1812.

ERRATA.

Page 63, line 27, *for* considerations, the evils found by experience to be such as *read,* considerations, such as the evils found by experience to be.

Page 109, line 12, *for* appointment of agents for the private trade in India, farther than by licence, *read,* appointment of agents at home for the management of the private trade from India.

Page 144, line 3, *for* £345,013, *read,* £41,946,

CONSIDERATIONS,

&c.

THE little interest taken in this country about the affairs of India, is matter of wonder as well as of regret. The consequence of general indifference upon the subject has been general ignorance; and though at the present conjuncture, when the attention of the Legislature is about to be drawn to the framing of "such measures for the future go-"vernment of the British possessions in India, as "shall appear from experience and upon mature de-"liberation to be calculated to secure their internal "prosperity, and to derive from those flourishing "dominions the utmost degree of advantage to the "commerce and revenue of the United Kingdom,*" dormant interests have been awakened and powerfully excited; it is yet to be feared, that under the existing want of information, the most dangerous errors will be committed, unless much wisdom and caution are applied to repress fallacious hopes, as well as to harmonize jarring pretensions and reconcile conflicting claims.

---

* Speech of the Commissioners at the opening of last session of Parliament.

There are certain general principles, from which it is presumed that no one will be found to dissent. Of these the most obvious are, that the common good of the empire in Europe and in Asia ought to constitute the basis of the new arrangement; that as no partial interest should be exclusively consulted, every partial view of the question ought to be received with circumspection, and even with suspicion; that subordinate ought to yield to paramount considerations; and above all, that experience should be trusted rather than speculation, in modelling the government and adjusting the relations of states.

The application of these principles to the present occasion, would naturally lead to an investigation of the causes which have produced the extension and consolidation of our power in India, and of the mode in which that power is exercised in the internal administration of those populous and fertile regions which now acknowledge the British authority.— There is hardly any question connected with the military and civil policy, the jurisprudence and financial economy of nations; scarcely any circumstance affecting the stability of governments, or the security, happiness, and prosperity of their subjects, which this range of inquiry would not embrace. Whether owing to the frequent discussions that have taken place in Parliament upon the system of administration introduced and acted upon by the East

India Company, all these questions are considered as finally put to rest, and a sound and matured conviction has been impressed upon the public mind, that both in principle and practice the system is upon the whole as unobjectionable as it can be made; or whether it arises from a prevailing indifference to unseen events and matters of remote interest, the attention of the country seems to be exclusively directed to the channel in which *the trade* with India is in future to be conducted. The state of existing treaties in India, the means and motives of aggression possessed by rival powers, the resources of wisdom and force by which aggression may be prevented or repelled, the constitution of the government, the regulations under which justice is administered, and revenue collected, and the different plans which have been proposed, or may still be in agitation for improving the condition of a vast population of British subjects, are studiously thrust into the back-ground, and in the controversy, as it presents itself in most of the publications of the day, we only see the East India Company endeavouring to preserve their commercial privileges, and another set of merchants struggling to invade them.

Were the question at issue really what in these publications it appears to be—one simply of a commercial nature—the writer of these pages would probably have abstained from taking any part in the discussion; and he has no hesitation in acknowledging, that could he bring himself to view the subject in the light in which it is vulgarly contemplated, merely as a contest between the East India Company and the great body of British merchants, for an improvable branch of commerce, as a dispute between expiring privilege and nascent right—the claimants of an open trade should have his hearty good wishes in the cause for which they are contending. In the whole confederated host of petitioners, against the Company's privileges, there is not to be found a more zealous advocate for commercial freedom, or a more decided adversary on general grounds to monopoly, than the individual who now ventures to submit his sentiments to the public. But strong as is the popular dislike to monopoly, there are evils which it would be still more imprudent to encounter; and however just may be the general partiality to liberty of trade, there are considerations entitled to a preference. Incompatibility between objects equally desirable, leaves only a power of choice, and this choice, if judiciously made, must be directed by a comparison between their practical utility, rather than their abstract fitness. The laws by which trade is regulated, form undoubtedly a prominent feature in national policy, but they have been usually held subordinate to those institutions which provide for the security of states, and the maintenance of their mutual relations. Foreign possessions are sometimes of immense importance in a political, and comparatively of small value in a commercial view,* and trading restrictions which if generally applied, would be unnecessary and noxious, may in certain cases be found both salutary and requisite.

It is not intended to make any attempt to prove that political advantages result to Great Britain from the empire which she has acquired in India. The fate of a country which has been the scene of so many triumphs to her arms, where the imperishable records of her virtue and humanity, as well as of her genius and enterprise appear, where the ashes of the best and bravest of her sons repose, can never be an object of indifference to England until she has ceased to care for all that concerns her glory.† Nor is it proposed to analyze the merits of the plan under which the affairs of India at

---

* The charges of the Bombay Presidency, exceed the revenues by more than a million sterling annually; but it surely does not follow, that on this account the settlement should be abandoned.

† It would be difficult to apologize for all the British transactions in India, since the year 1756; but dating from the time of Lord Cornwallis, it may safely be affirmed, that the spirit of the Company's policy has been wise, liberal, and humane. It exhibits an excellent practical comment upon the decree of the Roman senate, respecting Macedonia and Illyricum.—Omnium primum liberos esse placebat Macedonas atque Illyrios, ut omnibus gentibus appareret, arma Populi Romani, non liberis servitutem, sed contrà SERVIENTIBUS LIBERTATEM AFFERRE; ut et in libertate gentes quæ essent, tutam eam sibi perpetuamque sub tutelâ Populi Romani

home and abroad are now administered. The practical success which has attended this plan is its best encomium, and furnishes the most satisfactory answer to the objections to which in theory it may be open. The writer's views are much more limited. The value of our Indian empire, though perhaps underrated, is no where denied, and in so far as one can judge from the printed correspondence between His Majesty's Ministers and the Court of Directors, it does not appear to be in contemplation to make any material alteration in the constitution of the existing government, or in the distribution of the power with which its several members are clothed. The object of the numerous petitions which in the course of the last year have been presented to Parliament, is to procure for the merchants of the United Kingdom, indiscriminate and free admission into the trade with India and China, in derogation of the exclusive, or rather of the modified privileges now enjoyed by the East India Company, and this object to a considerable extent has received the countenance of His

---

esse; et quæ sub regibus viverent, et in præsens tempus MITIORES EOS, JUSTIORESQUE RESPECTU POPULI ROMANI HABERE SE. The decree was an excellent one, though it was lamentably executed. How proudly may the benefits conferred by Lord Cornwallis on the provinces of Bengal, Behar, and Orissa, and afterwards extended by Lord Wellesley to the people of the Carnatic, be contrasted with the conduct of Flaminius and Paulus Æmilius to the states of Greece!

Majesty's Government. It will be the writer's aim to shew, that this pretension, although ostensibly it be purely commercial, is in its bearings big with political mischief, and that, whilst it would, if sanctioned, utterly fail in obtaining for the petitioners the advantages they expect from a decision in their favor, it would prove ruinous in its operation to the general and paramount interests of the empire. To exclude political considerations from the discussion, would lead to participation in the prevailing error, but it is not meant to pursue them farther than is necessary to the exposure of that error.

Before entering upon any of those points of detail, which arise out of a subject confessed to be extremely extensive and complicated, it will not be either irrelevant or useless to advert shortly to the actual situations of the different parties whose interests are to be brought before Parliament for solemn deliberation and decision.

These interests may be arranged under three general heads—1st. The commercial and manufacturing interests of this country. 2dly. The political and commercial interests of the East India Company; and 3dly. The interest of Government so to conciliate and regulate the other two, as to render them conducive to the substantial and permanent prosperity of the empire. Let us look then, for a moment, to the situation in which the parties supporting these different interests are placed, regarding the approaching expiration of the East India Company's Charter.

1st. It is well known that from causes originating in the present convulsed state of the world, the pressure upon the manufacturing and mercantile classes of the community is severe beyond example. Reduced to circumstances of great difficulty and embarrassment from the want of markets for their produce, they look with eagerness to the opening of a trade, in the prosecution of which they would have little to dread from hostile annoyance. Those countries which have been acquired by the wisdom of the national councils, and by the vigour of the national arms, they naturally consider as the proper field for commercial enterprise; and in the vast resources of widely extended regions, they fondly anticipate the reward of industry, perseverance, and skill. Asia presents itself to their imaginations unlocking new and exhaustless stores for their acceptance, with a population of countless millions inviting them, with outstretched arms, to supply their unsatisfied and insatiable wants. Is this the present state of the public mind throughout the country, or is it not? and is it, or is it not a prospect which must prove fallacious? No one who reads the resolutions which have lately been passed in many of the manufacturing and trading towns, can doubt the fact of such expectations being entertained; and no one who has soberly meditated upon the information which is within the reach of all, and the accuracy of which is not liable even to suspicion, far less those who are accurately informed from experience and observation, respecting the constitution of Asiatic Society and the state of manners in that part of the world, can help being astonished that ideas so extravagant should have gained possession of the minds of any class of individuals usually distinguished by habits of accurate discrimination and calm reflection.

Much allowance is indeed due for the circumstances under which these visionary prospects are cherished, but the *tone* in which the claims of the respectable bodies alluded to are set forth, can hardly be considered as entitled to much indulgence. Their resolutions and petitions are couched in terms of bold and imperious demand. Apparently unconscious of danger from great and sudden innovation upon a system sanctioned by the experience of ages, they plead for its overthrow on the ground of indefeasible right long lain in abeyance. Capital embarked, property acquired, and services performed under the established system, are all to give way to speculative notions and theoretical plans, or at best to principles, which, however true in the abstract, are totally inapplicable to the service into which they are forced.

The pretension itself with the expectations founded upon it will be examined hereafter: the only inference meant to be deduced from these observations *now* is, that the claims of any set of men acting under the influence of great hardships, anxious for relief from every quarter whence relief can come, and even looking for succour where it is altogether unattainable, or attainable only by inflicting calamities greater than those they seek to alleviate, ought to be listened to with extreme caution.

2. The representations of the East India Company, as a party, likewise require to be scrutinized before being admitted. They have been invested with an important stewardship, and confirmed in it by no fewer than sixteen solemn acts of the legislature. Of this stewardship they are now called upon to render an account. If they have been negligent or unfaithful, let them be dismissed with indignity from the office: but though they even stood convicted of mismanagement, it would not follow that the principles on which the affairs of India have been administered, and the connexion between the two countries has hitherto subsisted, ought to be abandoned. A casual abuse of trust, though it may discredit the agents in whom confidence has been reposed and authority vested, does not necessarily impeach the system under which misconduct has taken place.—If on the other hand the Company have acquitted themselves in their high trust, not only with integrity and credit

to themselves, but with honour and advantage to the country—if they have done more with smaller means than ever was achieved by any other body, commercial or political, in the history of the world—if by encouraging the industry, and patronising the talent of their fellow-citizens, they have acquired and preserved an empire forming the brightest jewel in the British Crown—if they have improved the condition of their subjects in the same degree that they have extended their own jurisdiction—if in war they have shewn themselves to be a most powerful ally of the paramount state, and in peace a nourisher of its resources —if their mercantile gains have been uniformly and cheerfully sacrificed to the great objects of national security and national glory—if so far from acting in the hard character of exclusive monopolists, they have long since consented to a relaxation of the terms of their existing charter, by admitting competitors into their trade—and if unwilling to follow, or imitate the grasping spirit of their opponents, they have now signified their readiness to agree to every latitude being given to a commerce (established with their capital and by their exertions) that may be deemed compatible, not with the paltry consideration of a per centage, more or less, upon their mercantile investments, but with their duties as delegated Sovereigns, with the tranquillity of their possessions, and the consequent integrity and stability of the empire —surely an assembly exercising legislative functions, will listen patiently, and listen favourably also to claims fortified not more by prescription than by high desert.

The circumstances in which the Company appear before Parliament, soliciting the renewal of their charter, are rather unfavourable. The services that they have rendered to the state do indeed fill the most brilliant pages of its history during the last sixty years, but the public, from familiar acquaintance with most of these exploits, have ceased to be dazzled with their lustre. The gradual accessions of power, of wealth, and of revenue, which have been derived from India, are regarded by the nation as forming part of its own constituent resources, while the instrument by which these resources have been created, enlarged, and upheld, is too frequently overlooked. To superficial observers (and to this class, unfortunately, a majority of mankind will always belong) the recent applications of the Company to Parliament, for assistance under temporary pecuniary embarrassments, no doubt bear an unfavourable aspect. And lastly, a great establishment, like that of the East India Company, the Directors of which possess considerable power and patronage, naturally attracts some portion of envy and jealousy, feelings which, though strongly excited by the distresses of the times, are not so blind from their violence as to incapacitate those actuated by them, from availing themselves of all the difficulties in the Company's present situation, or from employing against it, with sufficient dexterity, those weapons of attack against trading monopolies, of which there is ample store in the repositories of economical science. For some of those unfavourable circumstances the Company are obviously not accountable; and if, as is hoped, it shall afterwards appear that for others they are not to blame, it behoves those who by careful investigation have become acquainted with their concerns, to shield them against vulgar obloquy, instead of joining in the clamour by which they are assailed.

3. In reference to the interest of Ministers, and to the arrangement which they may think proper to propose to the Legislature, for the double purpose of regulating the foreign and domestic government of our Asiatic possessions, and the mode of conducting the trade with India and China, they may be considered as liable to error, either from a consciousness of strength and a desire of increasing their own power and influence, or from a sense of weakness and a wish to strengthen themselves by the adoption of popular measures. In 1783, when the affairs of the Company were brought into discussion, it was contended by the ministry of the day, a ministry powerful from the talent and rank of its members, that the sovereignty of British India ought to be assumed by the King in right of conquest, and that the administration, in all its branches, ought to be intrusted to his responsible advisers; that all orders regarding the political, financial, judicial, and military autho-

rities in India, should emanate from the sovereign, and that the Company's territorial possessions should be governed on the same principles and in the same manner as the other dependencies of the crown. It was argued on the other hand, that such a scheme went completely to subvert the balance of the constitution by throwing the whole patronage of India into the hands of the crown; that by despoiling the East India Company of a property legally acquired, and to which they had an indisputable right of possession, it was repugnant to the dictates of common justice; and that if carried into execution, it would loosen and perhaps break the tenure by which these territories were held, by an injudicious application of European maxims of government to a country not more remote in situation, than dissimilar in usages from Great Britain. The plan, after being reduced into the shape of Bills, passed the House of Commons, but was thrown out by the other House of Parliament, and its rejection was signalized by the fall of the minister by whom it was introduced. The fate of these celebrated bills will, it is hoped, operate as a salutary warning to the present and all future administrations, against harbouring projects of ambition, similar to that, which at the period referred to, was not more fortunately counteracted than it had been imprudently disclosed.

Since the institution of the Board of Commissioners for the affairs of India in 1784, His Majesty's

Government have exercised, under the sanction of the Legislature, a general superintendence and control over the civil and military concerns of the Company; an interference which has occasionally been productive of inconvenience, but which, upon the whole, has tended to give stability and vigour to the system, and to preserve a harmony of view and pursuit, as to the great objects of national policy, without depriving the Company of the management of their trade, infringing their territorial rights, or arming Ministers with a degree of influence incompatible with the liberties of the people or the independence of Parliament. The opinion of His Majesty's present Government upon the merits of the system as it now stands, may be collected from the following passage in the letter addressed by Mr. Dundas (the late President of the India Board) to the Chairman and Deputy Chairman of the East India Company, under date the 28th Dec. 1808. "I have not yet "heard or read any arguments against the continu-"ance of the system under which the British posses-"sions in India are governed, of sufficient weight to "counterbalance the practical benefits which have "been derived from it, in their increased and increasing "prosperity, and the general security and happiness of "their inhabitants. It is possible that the same effects "might have been produced under a government im-"mediately dependant on the crown: but for the "attainment of those objects, the experiment is at "least unnecessary, and it might be attended with "dangers to the constitution of the country, which, "if they can be avoided, it would be unwise to en- "counter. Any alteration, therefore, which may be "suggested in this part of the system, will probably "be only in the details."* This language is perhaps more cautious than the occasion required: it is certainly much less decisive than what the late Lord Melville was accustomed to use, when, on the same topic, he thought it necessary to declare an opinion. It should, however, in candour, be recollected, that Mr. Dundas, in this very letter, had a communication to make to the Chairman and Deputy Chairman of the views entertained by Ministers on the policy of opening the trade with India which he knew would be most unpalatable to the Company, and that in order to pave the way for that proposition he just insinuated the *possibility, with some danger indeed to the Constitution,* (heaven save the mark!) of another plan being devised for the conduct of the government, on the old maxim which probably both he and they understand, "Better half a loaf than no bread." A more palpable and alarming hint, was indeed conveyed in the same letter,

---

* Printed Papers, p. 12.

The printed papers referred to, in this and other parts of the pamphlet, are the papers respecting the negociation for a renewal of the East India Company's exclusive privileges, printed by order of the Court of Directors, for the information of the proprietors of East India Stock, 4to Edition. When other documents are referred to, they are particularly specified.

respecting an alteration of the military system in India, and the consolidation of the Company's troops with the King's army; but the President of the Board seems to have been fairly reasoned into a retractation of this suggestion, by the letter from the Chairman and Deputy, dated the 13th January, 1809;* and Lord Melville, in his answer of the 17th December, 1811, after having had nearly two years for reflection, admits the objections to such a change to have great weight, and proposes to defer all farther discussion upon the subject until a future opportunity.†

Certain details, affecting both the civil government and the army, are left open for adjustment:‡ and

---

* Printed Papers, page 33. † Printed Papers, page 45.

‡ " In submitting to you these observations, however, I beg to be " distinctly understood as conveying to you only the PRESENT *senti-* " *ments* of His Majesty's Government on the SEVERAL POINTS *to which* " *the propositions relate.* Public discussion on such an important " question may possibly produce an alteration of opinion on some of " the details; and though the subject has been fully considered, it " may be deemed necessary in the further progress of the measure, " to propose on some points regulations of a different description " from those which are suggested in the enclosed observations:"

" ——— ——— ——— "Though various regulations may " possibly be necessary with a view to promote the discipline and " efficiency of the army in India, I am not aware that any legislative " enactments are requisite, *except as to the amount of force which His*

care must be taken lest these modifications as they may be termed, do not involve changes of great moment, which being sometimes effected under plausible pretences, and very modestly introduced into the world, are found on better acquaintance to assume a most imposing mien. But upon the whole it may be supposed with some degree of safety, that Ministers have no matured and deep-laid plan for materially altering the constitution of the Company, with any view of augmenting their own patronage and power.

The errors of weakness are, however, not less to be dreaded than those of ambition. The progress of the latter is sometimes staid by the re-action which they produce against their authors: the former springing from delusion, or from fear, flow on till their source is exhausted, and the mischief they occasion is irreparable. Encroachment is the cardinal vice of absolute governments. A spirit of unwise concession is the sin which more easily besets the ministers of a free state. Power is the object of both; the mode of pursuit is different; but the result is alike prejudicial to

---

" *Majesty may be empowered to maintain in India, at the expense of the* " *Company,* and perhaps also some provisions in regard to THE RELA- " TIVE POWERS OF THE BOARD OF COMMISSIONERS, AND THE COURT OF " DIRECTORS."—*Letter from Lord Melville to the Chairman and De-* " *puty Chairman, dated* 21*st March,* 1812.—*Printed Papers, pages* " 79 *and* 80.

the general weal. The application of these remarks will readily suggest itself to every one who has attended to the progress of the negotiation between His Majesty's Government and the Court of Directors, and to the occurrences, as well recent as more remote, which may be supposed to have retarded its termination.

Until the year 1793, the Company's exclusive trade was strictly guarded by legislative enactments; and, except in the indulgence granted to the commanders and officers of the Company's ships, no British subjects were allowed to embark in the Indian trade, although by special permission of the Court of Directors, goods belonging to individual merchants, had for a few years before that period been occasionally taken on board their vessels. By the act of 1793, the Company were bound to provide at a reasonable price 3,000 tons of shipping or more, annually, for the use of any of His Majesty's subjects who might be disposed to export British manufactures or produce to that extent, and to bring back returns in goods from India. The principal, if not the sole object of this clause in the act, was to transfer to the Thames the trade then clandestinely carried on between the British possessions in India and foreign Europe, by providing a legal channel through which the fortunes acquired by British residents in the East might be brought home to their native country.* At that period there were no vessels in existence, or in contemplation, for the Indian trade, except the regular ships of 800 tons burden employed by the Company.

The merchants and manufacturers of this country seldom availed themselves of the privilege which they acquired under the act of 1793: but in the course of the two or three following years some of the Company's ships were required by His Majesty's Government for the public service; and a scanty harvest having about the same time enhanced the price of bread, it was deemed advisable to import large quantities of rice from India, in any fit ships that could be procured either there or in England, liberty being granted to these ships to carry out cargoes from England to India. These circumstances led to the introduction into the trade between the two countries of a new description of vessels of small size, and cheap outfit, many of which were built in India, and navigated by Indian seamen. As the emergency which called these ships into employment was of a temporary nature, it would have been unreasonable after it had ceased, to give them a preference over the ships that had been built at home,

* A professed object was also to open a vent for British manufactures. See Act 33d George III. Cap. 52. Sect. 83.

and equipped expressly for the service of the Company, and which the Company were under engagement to employ for a stipulated number of voyages.

The Indian merchants, who were also ship-owners, seeing the prospect closed, which a temporary exigence had opened to them, complained loudly of the rate of freight and other grievances to which they were subjected by the Company's regulations, and as a relief from these hardships they prayed for the permanent admission of India built ships into the trade. Their representations occasioned a great deal of discussion both here and in India; and in 1802, after much deliberation, a final arrangement was made by the Court of Directors, with the sanction of His Majesty's Government, for the future regulation of the privileged trade between India and Great Britain.

It was then determined, that in addition to the three thousand tons of shipping allowed by the 33d of the King, a farther quantity of three, four, or five thousand tons, or as much as might be wanted, should be provided by the Company, and that the ships, without being diverted to political or warlike purposes, should be appropriated to the use of the private merchants, and sail regularly at the proper seasons. Except saltpetre, and piece-goods, all articles might be laden upon these ships. The first exception was made obviously from political considerations, and the second has not been enforced by the Company. Light and heavy goods were to be properly assorted by the Company's officers, and as the Company were to be answerable for the freight to the owners, so they were of course to load the ships if the private merchants declined, and the *onus* of providing suitable dead weight or ballast, also rested with the Company. The ships so taken up might be built either in England or India, and in no case were the merchants to be charged a higher rate of freight than the Company paid. In point of fact it has uniformly been considerably lower.*

In framing this arrangement, a clear and fixed line was drawn between a trade in its nature colonial, and a trade of simple remittance. The first could only be created by transplanting capital from this country to India; and the late Lord Melville, who at that time presided at the India Board, perfectly coincided in opinion with the Court of Directors, that the recognition of such a principle would be not only subversive of the privileges, and even of the existence

---

* The loss estimated to have been sustained by the Company in supplying tonnage for the privileged trade, from the year 1795 to 1810 inclusive, is £444,293, that sum being the difference between the amount of the freight actually paid by the Company for the shipping so employed, and the amount received by them from the private merchants. *See fourth Report of the Select Committee of the House of Commons, on the Affairs of the East India Company, page 444.*

of the Company, but prejudicial to the interests commercial and political of the whole empire.—The second was amply provided for in the way that has been stated. It must be confessed that the arrangement did not prove satisfactory to the private British merchants resident in India, or to their agents in this country; nor was this to be expected, because their pretensions were really, though not avowedly, founded upon the principle of a colonial trade; a principle, however, the benefit of which they were desirous should be confined to themselves as a body, to the exclusion of the rest of their fellow subjects. They wished in fact to obtain for themselves a full share of all the Company's advantages, without participating in the expense, risk, and responsibility attending its vast establishments both foreign and domestic. Being disappointed in this object, they have not ceased bitterly to complain of the restraints, delays, and vexations to which they allege that they have been subjected, from what they call an arbitrary exercise and wanton abuse of the Company's authority. Not content with presenting their complaints in the shape of representations and memorials to His Majesty's Government, and the Court of Directors, they have in the course of the last four or five years made frequent appeals to the public in pamphlets, where every term of invective is employed against the Company, and the whole policy of our Indian system is virulently attacked. The effect produced by those publications has been different probably from that which was designed. For the merchants and manufacturers at large petitioned Parliament to throw open the trade entirely, thinking very justly, that if the Company's privileges were to be invaded, and any farther enlargement given to a valuable branch of commerce, they had as good a claim as some eighteen or twenty houses of Indian agency to share in its advantages. The established houses of agency observing that things were thus taking a turn still more unfavourable to their views than the system itself on which they had laboured to encroach, have earnestly petitioned against the extension of the trade to the outports, and have remained neutral upon the other points of the controversy. Such are the conflicting pretensions which His Majesty's Government have in the first instance been called upon to reconcile, and which will soon be brought before Parliament for ultimate adjustment.

The task imposed upon Ministers, under these circumstances, is invidious and difficult, and even the purest intentions on their part do not hold out an adequate security for its right performance. As servants of the public, it is their duty at all times to defer to the public opinion, when constitutionally expressed, in so far as is consistent with an enlightened and honest sense of the national interests. At a season of great commercial difficulty, it is peculiarly their duty to devise means of relief, care being taken that the medicine administered be not of a nature to aggravate, instead of alleviating the general distress. It is not, however, to be disguised, that the object of the petitioners is to subvert the fundamental principle of our Indian policy, and altogether to change a system sanctioned by prescriptive authority, and by long experience of its advantages; that the benefits which may result from the experiment are distant, precarious, and perhaps unattainable, and that the evils which may ensue from it, are at least equally probable and incalculably more important; that the same claims which are now brought forward have been preferred on former occasions, and rejected; that the number of the petitions, (many of them coming from places which have no direct interest in the question), together with the intemperate language in which some of them are drawn up, the industry that has been employed in collecting them, the active canvass among members of Parliament to support them, and the delegation of committees to watch the progress of the discussions, were strongly symptomatic of an intention amid the distractions of political parties, and on the supposed near approach of a dissolution of Parliament, to obtain by clamour and intrigue a measure which the petitioners despaired of achieving under a less commanding, or more temperate influence.

The embarrassment occasioned by these opposite considerations is sufficiently visible in the past stages of the negotiation. In the letter from Mr. Dundas to the Chairman and Deputy Chairman of the East India Company, dated the 28th December, 1808, it is stated to be "fit that the Court of Directors shall "understand distinctly, that he cannot hold out "to them the expectation that His Majesty's Minis-"ters will concur in an application to Parliament for "a renewal of any privileges to the East India Com-"pany, which will prevent British merchants and ma-"nufacturers from trading to and from India and the "other countries within the present limits of the Com-"pany's exclusive trade, (the dominions of the empire "of China excepted), in ships and vessels freighted by "themselves, instead of being confined as at present "to ships in the service of the Company, or licensed "by the Court of Directors."* Let this communication be compared with the following extract from Lord Melville's letter, dated the 21st March, 1812: "You will do me the justice to recollect, that in all "our discussions on this subject, both recently, and "on former occasions, the admission of the ships of "merchants in this country into the trade of India, "in concurrence with those of the Company, has "never been urged as a measure from which much "immediate benefit would, in my opinion, be de-"rived either to the country, or to the individuals "who might embark in the speculation; and I cer-

---

* Printed Papers, page 15.

" tainly am not without considerable apprehension " that at least on the first opening of the trade, the " public expectation as to the British territories in " India affording any considerable outlet for British " manufactures beyond the amount of our present " exports, may be disappointed."* On comparing these two passages, it appears that in laying down an open trade to India, as an indispensable condition of Ministers' recommending to Parliament the renewal of the Company's charter, the late President of the India Board stipulated for what he afterwards admitted would be of little immediate benefit either to the country or individuals; and after such an admission, it is difficult to avoid the inference, that in making the stipulation, he did not act from his own conviction of its utility. He rests the proposition indeed in both letters upon the inefficacy of the provisions under the act of 1793, for the trade of private individuals between Britain and India, which are stated to have been " the source of constant dispute, and to have entailed a heavy expense upon the Company, without affording to the public any benefit adequate to such a sacrifice." But is it not at least doubtful whether the regulations which both his Lordship and the Court of Directors agree to be necessary, in order to guard against the facilities afforded by the

* Printed Papers, page 79.

new plan to persons who may attempt to settle and reside in India without a license from the Company, or without the knowledge and sanction of the local governments, will not prove equally unsatisfactory to the merchants both of this country and of India, as those privileges have been which were granted to them by the act of 1793, and subsequently extended by the Court of Directors in 1802? Reasoning *a priori*, it seems much more easy to regulate a monopoly than an open trade. The principle of freedom, and the proposed restrictions, are like the iron and the clay in the toes of Nebuchadnezzar's image; they may cleave, but they never will incorporate.

Again, in Article 6th, of a paper entitled—"*Hints Approved by the Committee of Correspondence, &c.,*" and submitted to Lord Melville on the 3d of March, 1812, as the outline of a plan on which the Company's Charter might be renewed, it was proposed "that the whole of the Indian trade should be "brought to the port of London, and the goods sold "at the Company's sales, and be as at present under "the Company's management."* The same principle was distinctly contained in the letter from the Chairs in January, 1809, and was not then controverted by Lord Melville. In answer to this proposition, however, his Lordship observed, in a paper transmitted on the 21st of March, 1812, "the adop-

---

* Printed Papers, page 63.

" tion of the regulation suggested will probably " tend to the security and advantage of the pub- " lic revenue, in collecting the duties on all arti- " cles imported from the East Indies and China, as " well as other countries to the eastward of the Cape " of Good Hope."* The answer is cautiously worded, and it would be uncandid not to allow that it contained, or rather implied, a reservation, under which Government might ultimately withhold assent to the proposition of the Court, a reservation of which the increasing clamour and combination against the Company, has actually since induced Ministers to avail themselves. What the petitioners for open trade wanted in argument, they made shift to supply by the number, importunity, and contrivance of their delegated counsel; and on the 27th of April last, the Earl of Buckinghamshire, who had then succeeded to Lord Melville at the India Board, acquainted the Chairman of the Court of Directors, that " the representations which had been brought " before His Majesty's Government, had led them " to entertain an opinion, that they would best con- " sult the public interests, by not confining the im- " port trade from the East Indies to the Port of Lon- " don."† Now without presuming to insinuate that this change of opinion constituted any breach of faith towards one of the parties engaged in the nego-

---

* Printed Papers, page 82.

† Page 146.

ciation, it was surely not too much to expect, that a distinct communication should be made to the Court of the substance of those representations which had produced a bias on the minds of Ministers, contrary to that which they had entertained only five weeks before. Had the question involved merely the security of the revenue, Government might have claimed credit on the score of their own public duty, for the exercise of a due degree of caution in lending their countenance to any measure, by which the stability of the national resources could be endangered. But as the point at issue affected the profits of the Company equally with the duties payable to Government, it was reasonable that the Court of Directors should be consulted respecting the probable efficiency of the plan in agitation for the prevention of illicit trade, if a plan had really been digested for that purpose; and the circumstance of no such communication having been made, suggests a doubt whether any such scheme was actually matured.

Hence it appears, that the Court of Directors had no sooner consented to a partial sacrifice of their trade to public feeling, or as they very properly termed it, to public prejudice, than they were urged by fresh demands to farther concessions; and were they now to agree to the extension of the Indian trade to the outports of the kingdom, they might next be called upon to surrender the commerce with China.

In making these remarks, or any others which may be hazarded in the sequel, there is no intention whatever of blaming the conduct of Government, and much less of reflecting upon the two most respectable noblemen, who have been the official organs of conducting the correspondence of that Government with the Court of Directors. The present Ministers have acted probably in much the same way that others would have done in their place. If more has been imputed to popular influence than belongs to it, the easier it will be to retract any rash opinion which may have been given, and to proceed with caution to the completion of the arrangement; if, on the other hand, that influence has been as sensibly felt as it was powerfully exerted, an acknowledgment of the difficulties with which Ministers have had to contend will account for, and in some degree extenuate, mistakes, though it certainly does not preclude a deliberate investigation of any errors into which they may have been seduced or impelled.

The following paragraph in Lord Melville's letter of the 21st of March, 1812, contains a short summary of those errors. " As far as relates to the trade with " India and several other countries, included within " the limits of the Company's charter, the Court do " not appear to have succeeded in establishing the " proposition, that any detriment will arise to the " public interest, either in this country or in India, " or ultimately even to the interests of the Company

" themselves, from the introduction of private adven-
" turers. If the Company carry on their trade more
" expensively and with less activity and industry than
" British individuals, it is unjust to the country, as
" well as to the inhabitants of British India, that the
" exclusive monopoly should be continued; and in
" such a state of things, the trade is more likely to
" be advantageous to the country and beneficial to
" the individuals, in their hands than in those of the
" Company: but if the latter shall conduct it with
" skill and enterprise, and with due and unremitting
" attention to economy, the extent of their capital,
" and the superior facilities which they must continue
" to possess, of providing their investment in India
" at the cheapest rate, will undoubtedly afford them
" the means of successful rivalship with all other
" competitors."* The proposition which the Court had endeavoured to establish was; " that the unli-
" mited freedom for which some persons had of late
" years contended, would have *political consequences*
" more injurious to the power of this country and of
" British India, than the advantages anticipated by
" sanguine minds could compensate if those advan-
" tages were to be realized; and that, moreover, the
" expectation of such advantages is unfounded, re-
" sulting from general presumptions, which are con-
" tradicted by the nature of the Indian people, cli-
" mate, and productions, and by the experience of

* Printed Papers, page 80.

"more than two centuries."* If this be not the proposition alluded to by Lord Melville in the letter above quoted, he has chosen to leave out of sight that upon which the Court of Directors thought fit principally to rest their case. If he alludes to it and at the same time denies its truth, he less impeaches their judgment, than the opinions of the most eminent statesmen who have taken a part in the affairs of India, for half a century past, opinions sanctioned within that period by eight decisions of the Legislature.† From the way in which his Lordship contrived to get rid of the objections to the scheme in contemplation, which were contained in that proposition, one might be led to suppose that the Court of Directors had searched their earliest records for some musty maxim upon which to found a new-fangled pretension, or that they had dipped into the impure sources of oriental fable, to collect matter of groundless apprehension and visionary alarm, whereas their only aim, in their correspondence with His Majesty's Government, seems to have been to vindicate the policy of existing laws, and to defend the doctrine of the Constitution, in relation to the British possessions in India.

---

* Letter from the Chairman and Deputy, dated 13th Jan. 1809. Printed Papers, page 20.

† 17th George II. Cap. 17.—7th George III. Cap. 57.—9th George III. Cap. 24.—13th George III. Cap. 64.—19th George III. Cap. 61.—20th George III. Cap. 56.—21st George III. Cap. 65.—33d George III. Cap. 52.

The whole tenor of the letter from the Chairman and Deputy, dated the 13th of January, 1809, is in perfect unison with the principles maintained by the late Lord Melville, and with the sentiments which he was at pains to avow on all occasions, when the merits of our Indian system were brought into discussion. In a letter dated the 2d of April, 1800, and addressed by the Right Hon. Henry Dundas, as President of the India Board, to the Chairman of the Company, upon the subject of the private trade, he thus expressed himself. "I set out with disclaiming being "a party to those opinions which rest upon any general attack of the monopoly of the East India "Company, either as to the government or commerce of India. My sentiments, in that respect, "remain exactly the same as they were when I moved "the renewal of the charter in 1793; and if any "thing, I am still more confirmed in the principles "I brought forward at that time. That a direct interference by Government in the affairs of India, is "necessary for their stability and uniformity, I am "more and more convinced; but that the ostensible "form of government, with all its consequent extent "and detail of patronage, must remain as it now is, "I am persuaded will never be called in question by "any but those who may be disposed to sacrifice "the freedom and security of our constitution, to "their own personal aggrandizement and ill-directed "ambition. I remain equally satisfied as to the "propriety of continuing a monopoly of the trade

" in the hands of the East India Company. Those " who maintain the reverse, appear to me to be " misled by general theories, without attending to " the peculiar circumstances of the trade they are " treating of. *Viewing it as a mere commercial ques-* " *tion, I believe this proposition to be a sound one: and* " *if the trade were laid open, the supposed advantages* " *thence arising, are at best very problematical, and* " *would certainly be very precarious and short-lived.* " The same principles which prove the necessity of " the present form and mode of Indian government, " evince the necessity of the monopoly of trade. The " government and the trade are interwoven together, " and we have only to recur to a very recent expe- " rience, to learn the immense advantages which have " flowed from that connexion of government and " trade. By the commercial capital of the Company " at home, acting in connexion with the public re- " venues under their administration abroad, they " have mutually aided and administered to the wants " of each other, and the result has been the fortunate " achievement of those brilliant events, upon the " success of which depended the existence of the " government, the territorial wealth, and the trade " of India." After recommending that a proper channel should be provided for the remittance to Great Britain of the fortunes acquired by individuals in India, he proceeds: " If I am asked whether, in " stating this principle, I mean that the trade to and " from India, in the common use of the terms, ought

" to be free and open to all His Majesty's subjects in " India? I answer distinctly in the negative. The " nature of the Indian manufacture, and the imme- " morial habits of the manufacturers, exclude the " practical application of so indefinite a principle to " the export trade from India. The manufacture of " the finer and more valuable fabrics of India, have " always been produced by advances from the go- " vernment, or individuals for whose behoof those " fabrics are manufactured, and if the dealing with " those manufacturers was to be laid open to the " uncontroled competition of every individual, the " consequence would be a boundless scene of confu- " sion and fraud, and ultimately the ruin of the ma- " nufacturers themselves." * * * * * * " It " is immediately connected with the observations last " offered, to consider by what agency is the trade of " individuals in India to be carried on? If this " question was to be decided on the principles of an " open and free trade, the answer to the question " would be, that every individual should send out or " employ any agent he thought best to manage his " own business. But from what I have already stated " on the former point, you will anticipate my opi- " nion on this; namely, that no agent should be " employed in India, or permitted to reside there, " except with the license of the East India Company, " and subject to the control of such regulations, as " the habits, prejudices, and trade of the country " may render expedient. In addition to every other

" consideration, arising out of the peculiar nature of " the trade and manners of the country, there is one " decisive circumstance against the tolerance of every " unlicensed adventurer in India. It would rapidly " and insensibly lead to the settlement and coloniza- " tion of the worst kind of adventurers taking root in " that country, than which there could not be a " more fatal blow to the permanence of the British " power and pre-eminence in India. No principle " ought ever to be tolerated or acted upon, that " does not proceed on the basis of India being " considered as the temporary residence of a great " British establishment, for the good government of " the country upon steady and uniform principles; " and of a large British factory, for the beneficial " management of its trade upon rules applicable to " the state and manners of the country."

* * * * * * * " In some of the many specula- " tions I have heard, and the publications I have " perused on this subject, it is usual to ask in a tone " of complaint, if it is not unjust and unfair that the " merchants and shipping of this country, other than " the shipping of the East India Company, should " be excluded from a participation of that trade " which is allowed to the subjects of foreign nations?

" The statement at first sight may appear plau- " sible; but when examined to the bottom, it has " no solidity. In truth, it is only another mode of

" objecting to the monopoly of the East India Com-
" pany. If there are reasons of sound policy, why
" the Legislature has decided that the India trade
" should be carried on by a monopoly, it is because,
" viewing the interests of the public as one aggre-
" gate, it is of opinion, that those interests are best
" cared for by that mode of conducting the trade.—
" Those, therefore, who state this objection, being
" themselves part of that whole, are, in common with
" the rest of His Majesty's subjects, reaping the be-
" nefit of that influx of national wealth and capital
" which the East India trade, so conducted, brings
" into the national stock. They cannot, therefore,
" more than others, because their occupation hap-
" pens to be that of merchants or ship-owners, com-
" plain of being injured by the means which the
" wisdom of Parliament has devised for introducing
" that flow of wealth into the kingdom.

" The case is totally different with regard to the
" subjects of foreign nations. They are not the
" objects of the care of the British Legislature;
" neither are their interests at all in the view of its
" provisions. They reap no benefit, but the reverse,
" from the growing wealth and prosperity of the
" British empire; and therefore are in no respect on
" a footing of comparison with any of the subjects of
" this country, to whom the restraints of the Com-
" pany's charter, for the reasons already assigned,
" do with perfect propriety apply.

" It is quite a separate question, how far it would " be right to hold our Indian possessions upon prin- " ciples of colonial monopoly? and it would be de- " viating from the strict matter of the objection, to " enter into that discussion in this place. It is suffi- " cient in point of fact to observe, in answer to the " merchants and ship-owners, that it is thought ex- " pedient for the interests of the empire at large, that " the East India possessions should not be regulated " on the principles of colonial exclusion; and there- " fore no part of the subjects of Great Britain can " be permitted to set up a separate interest of their " own against that general policy. If the colonial " principle was to be applied to the Indian territories, " it would not advance by one step that separate in- " terest set up by the merchants and ship-owners, to " which I now refer."

In reply to the question, Why the merchants and ship-owners, subjects of His Majesty, resident in Britain, should not have the same indulgences which are contended for by His Majesty's subjects resident in India? Mr. Dundas observed, " The answer is " plain and conclusive: in contending for this indul- " gence to the British subjects resident in India, I " am contending for a material national interest, " which is no other than this, that their fortunes, " capitals created in India, should be transferred " from that country to this, in a manner most bene- " ficial for themselves and the kingdom at large, in

" place of being transferred through the medium of " the commerce of foreigners, and thereby adding to " the wealth, capital, and navigation of foreign " countries. There is not a single circumstance in " which this applies to the case of merchants in this " country. It might be proved, if necessary, that " the only effect of giving such an indulgence to the " merchants resident in this country, would be a " temptation to withdraw a part of the capital of the " country, from a more profitable trade and more " beneficial application of it, in order to divert it to " another trade, less profitable to themselves and less " beneficial to the public. Without, therefore, one " single reason, either of private justice or public " policy, it would be introducing a rival capital in " India, against the remittance trade of the East " India Company, and in competition likewise with " those individuals whose capitals, by the proposed " indulgence, it is wished to transfer to Great Bri-" tain. It is argued that the extension of this indul-" gence to the British merchants, would be an addi-" tional encouragement to the export of British " manufactures. I need only observe that the argu-" ment proceeds on an erroneous view of the subject. " The export trade to India can never be extended in " any degree proportionate to the wealth and popula-" tion of the Indian Empire, neither can the returns " upon it be very profitable to individuals. Those who " attend to the manners, the manufactures, the food, " the raiment, the moral and religious prejudices of

" that country, can be at no loss to trace the causes " why this proposition must be a true one. The importance of that immense empire to this country, is " rather to be estimated by the great annual addition " it makes to the wealth and capital of the kingdom, " than by any eminent advantages that the manufactures of the country can derive from the consumption " of the natives of India. I do not mean to say that " the exports from this country have not been very " considerably increased of late years, and I make " no doubt, that from recent circumstances, they " may still be considerably increased. But the prospect, from the causes I have already referred to, " must always be a limited one, and I am positive that " the shipping and exertions of the East India Company, joined to the returned cargoes of those ships " which bring home the private trade of India, is " more than adequate to any present or future increase of export trade that this country can look " to upon any rational ground of hope." * * * * * * " With regard to the agents to be employed " at home, to manage the private trade of individuals " from India, and to take care of their interest in " the cargoes of the returning ships, I do not see the " use of any interference by the Company. *The " great interest to be attended to on the part of the " Company, is that no goods come from India that are " not deposited in the Company's warehouses, and that the " goods so imported are exposed at the Company's sales, " agreeably to the rules prescribed for that purpose.*"

On a perusal of the whole correspondence which took place between Mr. Dundas and a Committee of the Court of Directors in 1800 and 1801, it will be seen that there was a perfect agreement in principle, and a complete coincidence in general views, although there was a considerable difference of opinion upon some matters of detail. The President of the India Board had stated in the letter above quoted, the inadequacy of the provision for the private trade in the act of 1793, and urged the expediency of *allowing British subjects resident in India, to send home their funds in India built ships.* The Court professed their readiness to give every facility to the trade of remittance from India, but they contended that this, like the other branches of the trade, ought to be carried on through the medium of the Company's ships, and that the scheme for permitting British merchants resident in India, to introduce both their capital and ships into the trade, contained a principle of indefinite enlargement, which would gradually change the character of the existing intercourse. By the arrangement which took place in 1802, the difference was compromised, and India built ships were admitted into the trade, the Company reserving to themselves the power of freighting them, on private account. But before this arrangement was concluded, and while the discussion was still pending, it will appear from the following extract from Mr. Dundas's speech in opening the India budget for the last time in the House of Commons, on the 12th of June, 1801, that the difficulties which were started by the Court of Directors to some part of the measure recommended by him in the preceding year, had not in the least altered his sentiments and views respecting the constitution of the Company, or the general policy on which that constitution was founded, and by adhering to which it could alone be maintained. "Many objections have "been, from time to time, raised to the policy of the "restrictions imposed by the Legislature on the trade "of the East, and to the exclusive privileges placed "in the Company. My decided sentiments on this "subject are well known: I will therefore only now "advert to it, by observing, that at the renewal of "the charter in 1793, the Legislature shewed every "disposition to adopt such arrangements as might "secure to this country as large a share of the Indian "trade as possible. If any of the arrangements then "made, have been found by experience inadequate "to the object in view, the wisdom of the Legisla- "ture, and I trust a liberal and wise policy on the "part of the East India Company, will concur in "correcting former error. The manner in which "this shall be done, consistent with those regulations "which Parliament has thought proper to impose, "has long been under serious consideration. Many "indulgences have already been granted to indivi- "duals, and I have no doubt that ultimately such a "plan will be determined upon, as shall be the means "of affording all the satisfaction which in reason and "justice can be expected. In doing this, I certainly "do not mean to exclude every degree of proper "caution, for I have no hesitation in expressing my "thorough conviction of its being incumbent on "those with whom the final arrangement of this very "important branch shall rest, *never to lose sight of* "*those salutary maxims which have been prescribed by* "*long experience, and that they be strictly upon their* "*guard that substantial and permanent benefits may not* "*be sacrificed to casual and perhaps illusory schemes of* "*gain.**

---

* That these sentiments were not peculiar to the late Lord Melville, will appear from the following extract from a useful pamphlet, published by an officer of the India Board in 1793.

"On the grand point, that of opening the trade altogether, we "have as yet seen no specific, well-digested plan offered to the "public eye. It, however, can hardly be supposed, that even the "most zealous advocates for a new system, can be desirous of seeing "the present mode of conducting the trade determined, and "the future trade left *to hazard and chance.* A measure more "preposterous and absurd, nor any so fraught with ruin and "mischief to the general interests of the empire, as affecting "the *political*, the *mercantile*, and the *financial* concerns both of "*Great Britain* and *India*, could not be devised or imagined by an "enemy to both." * * * * * * "In this discussion we "have carefully avoided quoting any of the arguments used upon "former occasions for and against an exclusive trade, because by "the acquisition of kingdoms and provinces, the Asiatic trade has "since those times undergone an entire change, insomuch that "the order and system which formerly obtained in the conduct of "it, seem now to be perfectly inverted. The point contended for

Such were the opinions entertained by the late Lord Melville, after having devoted twenty years of a laborious life to the study of Indian affairs, and after having held for seventeen of those years the highly responsible office of President of the Board of Commissioners. He admitted, on retiring from office with the present Viscount, "that the system es-"tablished by the act of 1793, for the trade of in-"dividuals between Great Britain and India, had "not answered the expectations, or fulfilled the in-"tentions of the Legislature." Whether after the extension given to that system in 1802, he still re-

---

"on those occasions was simply mercantile. The subject now "spreads itself into a wider field: it attaches to it *political* concerns "of high importance as well as those of *commerce* and *finance*. At "those times a change in the existing system was of little compara-"tive consequence; the exports and imports were *small*, and the "revenue by customs, if it had suffered, could easily have been "made good; for the *National Debt* was then moderate, the objects "left for taxation were numerous; and the real and personal assets "of the Company, were more than sufficient after the discharge of "their debts, to make good the value of their capital stock; it "became therefore a question fairly determinable by the weight of "public opinion, how the India trade might be best conducted, "without involving in its consequences those important rights and "interests which seem now to depend on the continuance of the "present system of conducting the Government revenues and trade "in all its essential parts." *A Short History of the East India Company, and of their Trade to India and China, by Francis Russel, Esq.*; 2d edition, pages 41 and 45.

How much greater weight have not these considerations acquired since 1793?

mained of opinion, "that it did not afford all the sa-"tisfaction which *in reason and justice could be ex-"pected*," public documents furnish no means of judging. But every person who reads the above quotations with attention, must be persuaded that he never would have become a party to the proposition made by his successor as a *sine qua non* of the renewal of the Company's privileges "that *British merchants and "manufacturers* shall be permitted to trade to and "from India, and the other countries within the "present limits of the Company's exclusive trade, "(the dominions of the emperor of China excepted), "in ships and vessels hired or freighted by them-"selves, instead of being confined as at present to "ships in the service of the Company, or licensed by "the Court of Directors," far less that he would have concurred in the opinion more recently expressed, "that the legislature will best consult the "public interest by not confining the import trade "from the East Indies to the port of London." It is probable indeed, that he would not have dissented from the first proposition, in so far as it goes to put an end to the Company's agency in freighting ships for individuals, (an agency which it is equally probable the Company would not be indisposed to relinquish); but to the first part of the proposition we have his distinct negative upon record, as likely if acted upon, "to occasion a boundless scene of con-"fusion and fraud, and ultimately the ruin of the "manufacturers themselves; as tending to introduce

" without one single reason, either of private justice " or public policy, a rival capital in India, against " the remittance trade of the East India Company, " and in competition likewise with those individu- " als whose capitals it is wished to transfer to Great " Britain; in fine, as leading rapidly, though insen- " sibly, to the settlement and colonization of the " worst set of adventurers in that country, than " which there cannot be a more fatal blow to the " permanence of the British power in India." And in reference to the extension of the trade to the out-ports of the kingdom, we have also his recorded opinion, " that THE GREAT INTEREST to be attended to " on the part of the Company, is that no goods come " from India, that are not deposited in their ware- " houses, and disposed of at their sales."

During the whole course of the negociation, there is not to be found in the correspondence on the part of the Court of Directors, a single position which had not been advanced, and insisted upon by the late Lord Melville, as of primary importance to the interests both of the Company and the empire at large, nor is there any indulgence to the private trade which he thought it safe and expedient to grant, which the Court have not generally professed their willingness to concede. They have maintained with that experienced statesman, that a departure from the principle of the act of 1793, (by which the trade with India was placed under a regulated monopoly) is pregnant with political mischiefs, without affording the prospect of any equivalent advantage; while at the same time they have disclaimed "all narrow "considerations of commercial profit, or commercial "jealousy,"* and have announced "their readiness "to enter into a serious inquiry concerning the "concessions which can be made to the public, "without trenching upon the principles," not asserted for the first time in their letters, but "established in that act."† And the negociation seems to have been suspended in April 1812, in consequence of a difference of opinion between His Majesty's Government and the Court, not respecting a concession deducible from the principle of the act of 1793, but respecting an *extreme concession*, (the opening of the trade to the outports), arising altogether out of a *new principle*, and against which the Company had been specially warned by a distinguished member of an antecedent government, that it was *their great interest to guard.*

The writer, or rather the compiler of these sheets, (for hitherto they have consisted of little more than a compilation of the opinions of others), has formed too just an estimate of his own talents to be guilty of the presumption of supposing, that he can urge any thing effectual in the way, either of enforcing the arguments which have been employed by the

* Printed Papers, page 20. † Page 33.

Court of Directors, sanctioned as they have been by the concurrence of former Governments, and the past decisions of the Legislature, or of influencing the views of those with whom it will ultimately rest, to decide upon a great question of national policy. The short retrospect that has been taken of the relative situations of the different parties interested in the discussion, may however be useful; and though the observations that occur in the sequel, may not throw any new light upon the subject, still it is hoped that they will not be found altogether unworthy of attention by those who are disposed to candid inquiry.

In the early period of European intercourse with India, and previously to the acquisition of territory, the amount of the exports thither, in commodities from Europe, was very trifling. The investments for the home markets of the different nations engaged in the commerce were principally purchased with bullion, and almost all the *direct* advantage of the trade arose from the profits on the sales of those investments.* In proportion as territory was acquired,

---

* The following passage from Montesquieu, contains an apt illustration of this position, and indicates also the conclusion to which it leads. "Quoique le commerce soit sujet à de grandes revolutions, "il peut arriver que de certaines causes physiques, la qualité du "terrain ou de climat, fixent pour jamais sa nature.

"Nous ne faisons aujourd'hui le commerce des Indes, que par "l'argent que nous y envoyons. Les Romains y portoient toutes

the European residents increased, and of course drew from home a supply of commodities suited to their original habits and wants. But their numbers were

---

" les anneés environ cinquante millions de Sesterces. Cet argent, " comme le nôtre aujourd'hui, étoit converti en marchandises " qu'ils rapportoient en occident. Tous les peuples qui ont negocié " aux Indes, y ont toujours porté dês métaux et en ont rapporté dês " marchandises.

" C'est la nature même qui produit cet effet. Les Indiens ont " leurs arts, qui sont adaptés à leur manière de vivre. Notre luxe " ne sauroit être le leur, ni nos besoins être leur besoins. Leur " climat ne leur demande ni ne leur permet presque rien de ce qui " vient de chez nous. Ils vont en grande partie nuds, les vête- " ments qu'ils ont, le pays les leur fournit convenables; et leur re- " ligion, qui a sur eux tant d'empire, leur donne de la répugnance " pour les choses qui nous servent de nourriture. Ils n'ont donc " besoin que de nos métaux qui sont les signes des valeurs, et pour " lesquels ils donnent des marchandises, que leur frugalité et la na- " ture de leur pays leur procure en grande abondance. Les auteurs " anciens qui nous ont parlé des Indes, nous les dépeignent telles " que nous les voyons aujourd'hui quant á la police, aux manières " et aux mœurs. Les Indes ont été, les Indes seront ce qu'elles " sont à present; et dans tous les tems, ceux qui negocieront aux " Indes, y porteront de l'argent, et n'en rapporteront pas." *De* " *l'esprit des loix, Livre* xxi. Cap. I.

When the President Montesquieu wrote this chapter, he did not foresee the change that has taken place in the commerce between Great Britain and India resulting from the acquisition of territory, and the subsequent conversion of a trade of barter into a trade of remittance. But his remarks are strictly applicable to the grounds on which the private traders now rest their pretensions, and are also in direct opposition to their views.

comparatively so small that this demand, with all the warlike stores and clothing for the troops in the service of the European states, formed but an inconsiderable export. Rivalship in trade between those states at length begot political hostility, and the result of that hostility (whether fortunately or not, it is of little consequence now to inquire) has put Great Britain in possession of a vast Empire in Asia. It would indeed have been a barren conquest if it had afforded no rational prospect of rewarding, by some means or other, the toil and expense of acquiring, as well as the trouble and cost of administering and defending it. A *surplus Revenue* was expected from the Company's territories (obtained in part by purchase, in part by conquest, and in part by cession), after all the charges connected with the government and management of them were defrayed. This surplus, rendering unnecessary, or at least diminishing the former export of bullion from England, was to be realized through the channel of the homeward trade. Whether this expectation was reasonable or not, and whether, if reasonable, it has not been defeated by mismanagement, are fair and proper questions, but not the immediate subjects of inquiry. The statement, as it stands, serves various purposes. It shews, that prior to the possession of territorial dominion by European nations, the trade with India consisted in an exchange of its commodities for their bullion, not for European commodities; it shews that one of the expected effects of the acquisition of territory by this country, was a trade of remittance homeward superseding more or less the export of the precious metals; and it leads to a consideration of the system under which it has been at least attempted to establish that trade of remittance. The importance of each and all of these points is manifest, when we attend to the grounds on which the present expectations of the mercantile and manufacturing classes are founded, and to the radical change which an endeavour to gratify such expectations must necessarily induce into the whole system of our Indian policy.

The great source of the prevailing notions seems to be a mistaken idea, that our Asiatic territories present an advantageous market for British produce and manufactures. This idea probably originates in a natural though inconsiderate comparison of the general state of India with that of our American colonies, while in truth no two things can be more at variance. The islands in the West Indies are peopled by Europeans, having the same wants and habits with ourselves; by Africans in a state of servitude, which subjects them morally, as well as physically, to the will of their masters; and by a mixed race, whom necessity, constitutional bias, habit, and example, have inured to our mode of living. Almost every thing that the joint population consumes and uses is sent from this country; their clothing, great part of their food and drink, their household furniture and utensils, their trinkets and ornaments, their instruments of cultivation, the harness for their horses, mules and cattle, and the machinery for the manufacture of their raw produce. The planter unites in himself the several characters of a cultivator, a manufacturer, and a merchant; and in all these capacities he is more dependent on the mother country for supplies, than she is upon returns from her colonies.—How different the state of India! There a fertile soil yields every thing necessary to supply the wants and to conduce to the comfort of its inhabitants; a refined and ingenious people, have long since carried many of the arts to a still unrivalled pitch of perfection; their manners and civil institutions, grafted upon and combined with their religious tenets, are immutable because they are sacred; the same occupations and professions have descended in the same families during a lapse of ages, in a line of undeviating succession; the artificial distinction of castes has erected barriers between the different classes of society, which it is impossible to break down or overpass. The division of labour, which has contributed so much in Europe to mechanical improvement, is not only practically unknown to the natives of India, but is incompatible with their prejudices and customs. Their domestic economy is as unchangeable as their geographical position upon the face of the globe. They want nothing from us, and many of the superfluities with which we could furnish them, their religion has taught them to abstain from, or to hold in abhorrence. Even the demand for the finer sort of woollens, which used to be in considerable request while the native courts were in their splendour, is sadly impaired, and the little that remains is now confined entirely to the Company. This state of things we cannot change, and as it is impossible to fashion circumstances to our policy, we must be contented to accommodate our policy to the circumstances in which we are placed. Hence it follows, that the commodities exported from India must be purchased there by the precious metals, as was anciently the practice, or be remitted, conformably to the present system, in the shape of tribute, or surplus revenue, or in the fortunes of individuals, realized in the course of administering the various branches of the Government.

Whether any country can for a long period of time afford to yield a considerable tribute without receiving a commercial return, in one form or other, is a curious question of political economy; and those who are disposed to support the negative of the proposition, will have some difficulty in shewing the utility of our territorial acquisitions in India. If it is impracticable in the present channel to realize a perpetual tribute, it will be equally so in any other channel through which it may be attempted. The difficulty will neither be obviated nor lessened by transferring the right of conveyance from the East India Company to the great body of British Merchants, and the question for Parliament to deliberate and decide upon will be, not how the trade shall be carried on, but whether our possessions in India shall be retained or abandoned?

Those, on the other hand, who may be of opinion that the surplus produce of the land and labour of an extensive and fertile country, inhabited by a numerous and industrious population, can afford to pay for security, the equal distribution of justice, and the various advantages emanating from a vigorous and enlightened Government, will probably admit that all the trouble, expense, and responsibility should *not* be imposed upon one class, whilst all the benefit is allotted to another class of individuals; that the East India Company should *not* be loaded with all that is burdensome in the Indian connexion, if they are to be excluded from the fair recompense of capital, enterprise, and laborious management.

It has been urged with more confidence than candour, that it is idle to talk of a surplus revenue from our Indian territories; that none of the promises that have been made on this subject in time past, have ever been fulfilled; and that any expectations which may now be held forth will be productive only of new disappointment. But before coming to so hasty a conclusion, let it be recollected that the East India

Company had been for a long period incessantly engaged in expensive wars, both in India and in Egypt; that these wars have terminated successfully for the Company, and gloriously for the country; that it has been subjected to a great expense in fitting out expeditions for the reduction of the Eastern settlements of the European enemies of Great Britain; that by the prosperous issue of these expeditions, the dominions of the Crown have been extended, and England left without a rival in the whole southern hemisphere. Let it also be considered, that peace in India is now established upon a foundation which promises to be permanent; that whilst the Company's debts do not much exceed twenty-eight millions, its annual revenues amount to considerably more than fifteen millions sterling—that this revenue is collected with greater ease and punctuality than the same sum is realized in any country under Heaven, the balance remaining unacquitted at the end of three months immediately following the close of the official year (as appears from documents before the public*), not exceeding a half per cent. in the old territories, and falling short of two per cent. in the provinces more recently acquired; that the beneficent effects of their mild system of administration, matured by

* Second Report of the Select Committee of the House of Commons, on the Affairs of the East India Company, ordered to be printed 11th May, 1810.

experience, and consolidated by time, is attested by the increasing confidence of the natives, the progressive improvement of the agriculture and internal commerce of India, and a reduction of from two to four per cent. upon the interest of their debt. And after enumerating these considerations, the adversaries of the Company may safely be challenged to produce an instance in the history of the world, in which equal glory and equal advantage have been attained by equal means; where the sacrifices that have been made bear so small a proportion to the objects which have been secured, and where the burdens of the Government are so light when compared with its resources.

Nothing, however, tends so much to obscure the prospect before us, as the approach of hasty and inconsiderate innovation. It was by extreme caution and by rejecting every measure that wore an unknown aspect, that our power in India was obtained, and can alone be preserved. While the Company acted in the simple capacity of merchants, they confined themselves to their factories, occupied solely by the concerns of their trade. Even after acquiring territory, they did not venture to govern in their own name. During the existence of what was termed the double Government, the administration was conducted by natives of rank on behalf of the Company, but in the name of the Mogul. The direct appearance of the Company in the

Government is comparatively of modern date, and though the change has certainly been most beneficial upon the whole, yet but for the absolute control exercised by the local Governments over their own servants, as well as every European licensed to reside within their territories, it could not have failed to produce the most mischievous effects. The exercise of this control is easy or difficult, in exact proportion to the number over whom it is extended. Every thing bearing the semblance of arbitrary power, is so inconsistent with the principles, feelings and habits of British subjects, that it must always be submitted to by them with reluctance. Thus measures of indispensable precaution would, in certain circumstances, be represented by those affected by them, as insupportable grievances, and acts of heavy oppression. The imprescriptible rights of Englishmen would be pleaded against the mandates of authority; men having a common interest would make common cause; numbers would give confidence to the discontented, and a formidable opposition be arrayed against the government. Under the *native* Governments in their pristine vigour, such effects could never have been apprehended. They would have consulted their own interest by summary means, and paid little attention to the convenience or remonstrances of obnoxious individuals: but weakened as the sovereign authority in India already is to a certain degree, by the hands in which it is placed, it would be worse than imprudent, it would be foolhardy in the extreme to expose it to attack from a new class of settlers, difficult enough to be controlled even when they exist in small numbers, and who, if allowed to multiply, would break down all restraint.

It is well known that there is a class of politicians in this country, who treat these dangers as phantoms proper only to impose upon the weak and alarm the timid, and who are so little afraid of innovation as seriously to recommend the encouragement of colonization in India, instead of preventing its commencement and checking its progress. The persons alluded to, gravely contend that our Indian Empire must be a useless and burdensome appendage, until the plains of Hindostan are peopled by a race of European extraction, with their industry guided by British ingenuity, and stimulated by British capital. Independence they regard as the *euthanasia* of colonization; and in the ardour of their enthusiasm they view the separation of the American colonies from the parent state, and the consequences which have resulted from it to the new and the old world, as a happy omen of a revolution in Asia, proceeding from the same causes, and pregnant with similar results. These gentlemen, however, seem to forget that fifty millions of people stand in the way of their project;—that the present population must be extruded or exterminated before it can be carried into effect; —that this is an undertaking equally above our means and our warrant;—that the conduct of Spain in South America (from which, rather than from the policy of England, in the northern provinces of that Continent the precedent seems to be drawn) has hitherto excited more abhorrence than admiration,—and that if the scheme were as successfully executed as it is mercilessly conceived, the expectations founded upon it must inevitably be defeated by the universal tendency of men as well as of animals and plants, not indigenous to the climate of Asia, to degenerate, when transplanted thither, in the course of a few generations. In proof of the last proposition, an appeal might be made to the degraded condition of the descendants of the Portuguese and Dutch colonists upon the Coasts and Islands of India, but in opposition to all the reveries of these theorists, it will be sufficient to quote the practical wisdom of the late Lord Cornwallis.—" I am strongly impressed " with a conviction," says that venerable nobleman, in a letter to the Government at home, dated November 1794, " that it will be of essential importance to " the interest of Britain, that Europeans should be " discouraged and prevented as much as possible, " from colonizing and settling in our possessions in " India."

The grounds on which this opinion was formed were partially detailed in a letter from this eminent man to the Court of Directors, dated the 1st. of November, 1788, a document well worth the attention of the merchants of this country, as well as of the Legislature, at the present juncture.

" The exposition now given of the usual manner " of providing goods here, and of the consequent " restraints necessary upon manufacturers, serves to " point out what the true principle of *freedom of* " *trade* in this country must be. A great deal has " been said on the subject, and apparently in refer- " ence to the state of things in Europe, where in " every branch of manufacture there are opulent " men that work upon their own stock, and where " the markets, supplied by goods thus produced, " leave, as they ought, the seller and buyer per- " fectly unrestrained. But here the single circum- " stance of making advances to the manufacturer " creates a great distinction. It is hence necessary " to make regulations for preventing injustice, and " therefore, instead of *a freedom without limitation*, " to which some arguments have gone, it seems a " just idea of *true commercial freedom* in the circum- " stances of this country—that *all be allowed to trade,* " *but according to priority of engagements and advances* " *to receive their returns.*"

Upon a scheme which had been at different times suggested (and which never was more palatable than it is likely to be now) for abolishing the Company's commercial establishments, withdrawing the agents from the districts, and providing their investment with ready money at Calcutta, his Lordship, in the same letter, made the following observations :—" The " ascendency which the character and situation of " Europeans have given them over the natives, has " been already noticed, and the importance of the " Company's commercial establishments, in the hands " of their servants especially, has also been seen in " protecting the manufacturers and preserving the " fabrics, which purposes are more likely to be an- " swered in the hands of the Company's servants " than of other individuals. The fraudulent disposi- " tion, likewise, of the manufacturers has been ob- " served, and to these may be added, the still too " feeble operation of laws and regulations in places " distant from the seats of authority and justice. If " the proposed scheme were adopted, multitudes of " Europeans would flock into the interior parts of " the country—they would naturally possess them- " selves of the seats of the manufactures abandoned " by the Company—eager competition must imme- " diately arise—enhanced prices, and debased fabrics " follow—the weavers would receive advances from " all, and, probably, disappoint all—each would be " ready to take redress at his own hands—disputes " between merchants, as well as between them and " the manufacturers, would be inevitable—and the " country thus, in all probability, become a scene of " confusion and disorder, which the distant situation " and other avocations of the collectors would little " permit them to rectify. How far a salutary "freedom and extension of commerce would be "promoted by such means, it cannot be hard to "determine."

Though the foregoing extracts seem to present a mercantile view of the case only, they point to considerations of a general nature, which were strongly urged upon the attention of the authorities at home, in other despatches of the same virtuous and enlightened Statesman, as bearing directly upon the great question, *How the dominions which have been acquired for Great Britain in India can be best* PRESERVED? If in the progress of the approaching discussions this grand political question ever should be lost sight of, or if the primary object of *security* should eventually be made to give way to considerations of inferior moment, the evils that are likely to ensue it is easy to foresee, but dreadful to contemplate.

Generally speaking, the system under which possessions have been acquired, will be found the most effectual for their maintenance, particularly if that system has been so far matured as to provide for their consolidation and defence, their civil organization and internal quiet, their substantive resources and relative dependency. The policy of altering an established system may be influenced by various considerations, the evils found by experience to be such as attached to it, the power of correcting those evils without incurring the risk of greater mischief, the character and habits of the people governed, and a multiplicity of circumstances incident to the sovereign authority, in whomsoever vested. It is universally admitted, that innovations of every description are more hazardous in India than in any country on the face of the earth; and if one thing has contributed more than another to the preservation of British ascendency in that quarter, it has been a stedfast adherence to the principle of abstaining from all interference with the customs, opinions, and prejudices of the natives, and of proceeding with the utmost caution and deliberation in adopting the most obvious improvements; to a desire on our part to get acquainted with their manners, laws, and religion, solely for the purpose of testifying our respect for them; to a delicate regard for every thing that was wise and good; and a prudent forbearance with whatever appeared to be absurd or ill digested in their manners and institutions: in a word, it has been to firmness tempered by much accommodation in our deportment, and to plain dealing in our transactions, that we owe all that we have acquired; and it is only by persevering in the same line of conduct that we can hope to retain what we hold. This principle, however, could never have been acted upon with systematic uniformity, had no limits been imposed to the number of resident Europeans. Every government, in virtue of its constituent attributes of punishing and rewarding its own servants, may prevent gross abuses on their part, and even give a tone to the *manners* of those whom it employs; but it would be impossible for any government, however absolute, vigilant, and energetic, to watch, control, and regulate a numerous European population, dispersed over the widely-extended provinces of India. It will perhaps be urged that these observations are unnecessary, because there is no intention of permitting a free ingress of Europeans into our Indian territories. But it is of very little consequence that this is not the professed basis, if it shall prove the actual, though unavowed consequence of the new arrangement.

Liberty of trade presupposes every facility of carrying it on to advantage. It supposes that those who take cargoes to India shall have a choice of markets; that if they are disappointed at one place, they shall be allowed to transport them to another; that *there* they shall be permitted to remain until their transactions are finished, or rather until they choose *to confess* that their business is brought to a close; for it will be found quite impracticable to fix such a period for their stay, as in some cases will not give rise to hardship, and in others to abuse, and equally impracticable for the local authorities to inquire into the circumstances connected with each adventure. The making of purchases will involve still greater difficulties. Every person at all acquainted with India, knows that there are no stores of goods at the maritime ports from which cargoes can be made up. An order in long advance must be given for the goods which it is intended to export. Part of the price must be advanced before the raw material is manufactured, sometimes before it is in existence; another part must be paid before the article is delivered, and the remainder at the period of delivery. In India there are no over-stocked warehouses, no bills at distant dates, no twelve-months or two years' credit. Who then are to provide the investments of the private merchants? If the servants of the Company, a conspiracy would instantly be suspected to ruin the private merchant by supplying him with bad articles at exorbitant prices. If agents are to be chosen by the merchants themselves and permitted by the Government to reside in India, the most superficial thinker must perceive that this is a trade for which an apprenticeship is necessary, and that a young man sent out to India from Liverpool, Manchester, or Glasgow, ignorant of the language and manners of the natives, would require some tuition before he could be qualified to acquit himself with advantage of the trust reposed in him by his employers. The *number* of these agents, however, is a matter of much greater anxiety than their qualifications; and to their number no probable limits can be assigned. The same reason which would prevent the private merchants, as a body, from intrusting the Company's covenanted servants with the purchase of their investments, would make them distrustful of the agents selected by each other, and the only remedy seems to be, permitting every individual concerned in the trade to have his separate agent. The consequences it is easy to foretel. In the ardour of new adventure, the Indian market will soon be glutted with European produce (for at this moment it is overstocked), and the irritation resulting from disappointment will vent itself against the local governments, to whose restrictions the disappointment will be imputed. At present the *boon* only is contemplated, while the *conditions* annexed to it are overlooked.—*Then* the conditions will be represented as more irksome and vexatious, than the total exclusion from the trade had been. Every species of evasion will be practised, and open acts of disorder committed. The operation of the law will be eluded or set at defiance. A fertile soil peopled by a feeble and timid race of inhabitants, will tempt illicit enterprise. Those who cannot earn a subsistence by legitimate pursuits, and who have not the means of returning home, will try to live as they can, by fraud, by plunder, or by arms. The peaceable and defenceless natives will be harassed and exasperated till they are at last goaded on to resistance. All respect for the national character will be extinguished, and *opinion*, the only support of the Government, be converted into the instrument of its downfal. Popular discontent will be fomented and organized by the ambition of native chieftains, prompted and aided by the most intelligent of the

Europeans, who will seek refuge under their standards from the vengeance due to their crimes. Multitudes of idle, restless, and desperate people will flock to India from this and other countries, eager to repair their fortunes, or to attain unprincipled distinction; and instead of that fair monument which the valour, wisdom, and worth of fifty years have been labouring to rear to the fame of England, and the hallowed interests of humanity, we shall leave only the miserable traces of imbecility and discord, fields of desolation, and a pile of ruins!

These are indeed portentous reflections, and would to God they had no better foundation than in the forebodings of a gloomy or heated imagination. It happens unfortunately, however, for those who may wish to give a pleasant face to a grave subject, that they completely accord not only with the sentiments which have been expressed by every Governor of India, from Mr. Hastings down to Lord Minto, but with all past experience.*

---

* The emphatic language of Mr. Hastings ought never to be forgotten. "I much fear, that it is not understood as it ought to be, "how near the Company's existence in India has on many occa-"sions vibrated to the edge of perdition, and that it has been at all "times suspended by a thread, so fine, that the touch of chance "might break, or the breath of opinion dissolve it; and instantaneous will be its fall whenever it shall happen. May God in "his mercy long avert it!" *Review of the State of Bengal.* London, 1786. Page 154.

The commercial and political evils which must result from the influx of Europeans into India, the history of our own and other countries, may teach us duly to appreciate. Thus, when Cromwel, in the year 1655, withdrew his protection from the Company, a crowd of adventurers rushed into the trade; the prices of English commodities in India were immediately reduced, while the prices of Indian produce and manufactures rose in an equal degree. The adventurers were subjected to every species of insult and indignity by the native powers, who soon discovered that the people they were dealing with did not belong to the great Company which they had learned to respect. The fall in value of Indian commodities in England, arising from eager and sudden competition, brought ruin on many of the speculators, and left no other compensation to the country for a large capital uselessly employed, than the unnatural stimulus given to rapid and wasteful consumption by low prices and a glutted market.

Another remarkable instance of the mischiefs arising from the resort of private adventurers to India, occurred in the reign of Charles II. At that time a number of private ships embarked in the trade, in defiance of the Company; and though a few of the adventurers gained by the experiment, a very large proportion were ruined in consequence of it. Nor was this all—the officers and men conducted themselves during their stay in the country with so much arrogance and impropriety, as to excite the general indignation of the inhabitants, and to draw upon the nation the resentment of the Mogul and other native Princes. War was declared—the Company's factories were seized, and the complete extirpation of the English from India, after five years' interruption to their commerce, was with difficulty prevented by the interposition of the British Government, and the most rigorous measures against the interlopers.

The fate of the Portuguese power in the East, presents an awful warning to Great Britain. The intolerable license of the roving adventurers of that nation rendered them odious to the natives, and by arming against them the whole population of the coasts and islands of India, led to the final subversion of their power by the Dutch.

The records of the English East India Company abound with instances in which the liberty of residing in India, under all the limitations at present annexed to it, has been grossly abused. To select only one out of many which might be mentioned: in 1795, two persons of the names of Arnott and Bellasis, were ordered out of India for having furnished warlike stores to the Mahrattas. The former surrendered himself, or rather was delivered up, but the latter sought protection from one of the Bundela Chieftains, by whom he was afterwards employed in training and disciplining a corps of natives. About the same period, Sir John Shore was harassed with representations connected with the residence of a number of Europeans who had settled in the province of Oude, the Vizier complaining of their interference with his officers in the collection of the revenue; and the settlers, on the other hand, claiming protection from the Governor-General against the vexations practised upon them by that Prince. In short, it was to the influence possessed by Europeans over the councils of the Sultan of Mysore, and of the Mahratta Chieftains, that the almost incessant wars in India, for a period of fifteen years, are principally to be ascribed.

In reference to these serious and well-known facts, it is to be hoped, that the Legislature will be cautious in giving its sanction to any system of intercourse by which the political interests of the country may be compromised, and our connexion with India brought into peril. The value of the stake is immense, and if we transgress the rules of the game, although by some lucky hits, we might be successful for a time, the ultimate chances, according to all calculation, are against us.

The views of the petitioners against the Company's exclusive privileges, being directed to a participation in the China trade, as well as the Indian, it becomes necessary to inquire, what would be the probable effects of throwing open that branch of Asiatic commerce to the public at large. It will be seen on referring to the Hints submitted to the consideration of the late President of the India Board by the Court of Directors, and to the Observations sent in answer to those hints by Lord Melville,* that in the opinion of His Majesty's Government, it will be "advisable, with a view to the security of "the revenue, and to other objects connected with "the trade to China, to leave it on its present foot-"ing, and to guard by proper regulations against "any encroachment on that branch of the East India "Company's exclusive privilege." It may therefore be assumed, that on this point there is no difference of opinion, at least in principle, between His Majesty's Government and the Court of Directors.—The question, however, is one on which the public have a voice, and whatever agreement may be entered into between Ministers and the Directors, is subject to the future revisal of Parliament. If the public have been unfairly dealt with in any part of the proposed arrangement, an appeal lies open to the highest tribunal recognized by the constitution, a tribunal perfectly competent to reverse any preliminary judgment which may have been passed unfair towards the claimants, injurious to the East India Company, or prejudicial to the general interests of the empire. Every question connected with the subject, ought therefore to be treated upon the broad grounds of political and commercial expediency, without regard to the recorded opinions of any party in the pending discussion. The author

---

* Printed Papers, page 62 and 82.

is fully sensible of the disadvantage under which he labours, from want of access to any *special* source of information. His only apology is the consciousness of meaning well, his only encouragement under an acknowledged and lamented deficiency, proceeds from confidence in the public candour. The following facts, the authenticity of which may be depended on, will, perhaps, protect him from the charge of wilful ignorance, or remissness in seeking for information in those quarters where there was a probability of its being obtained.

They may be arranged, with reference first to the municipal laws and institutions of China; and secondly, to the manufacturing, commercial, and fiscal interests of this country.

I. Some of the peculiarities in the character of the Chinese Government and people, are necessary to be known before the nature of our connexion with the country, and the fickle tenure on which it depends, can be rightly understood. Their mode both of thinking and acting is marked with a strong dislike and contempt of strangers. Agriculture constitutes the basis of the economical policy of the government, and the favourite pursuit of the people. The advantages of foreign commerce, though better appreciated now than in time past, are still held in secondary consideration, whilst the jealousy which pervades and embarrasses all their intercourse with strangers, operates both as an obstacle to the extension of trade with their country in general, and as an impediment to the ordinary course of business with the natives, even upon its present restricted scale. Canton, or rather the river on which it stands, is now the only port in the empire open to foreign commerce. The European nations who have carried on the trade with China, never being permitted to settle upon the Continent, or to approach with their ships nearer than Hongpou, which is four leagues from the city of Canton, successively established factories on several of the little islands at the mouth of the river. To this day the English factory, after completing their sales and purchases at Hong, retire to Macao, a small settlement belonging to the Portuguese, afraid of awakening the suspicion of the Chinese Government, or of involving themselves in disputes with its subjects.

The system of absolute despotism, (in itself unfavourable to commerce) on which the Chinese Government is founded, and which pervades all the gradations of rank in society, has given rise to a notion from which no class in the country is exempt, that all communities, whether great or small, both in their integral masses and separate portions, are subject to the same mode and degree of authority as exists in China; that the Chief of the Company's factory possesses, or ought to possess, unlimited power over all individuals belonging to the English nation during their stay at Canton, and that he, as well in his person as in the property committed to his charge, is responsible for every infraction on the part of his countrymen of the laws of the empire.

For many years the Company's representatives possessed no legitimate control over any other than the ships of their employers under their immediate orders, and accordingly the inconvenience resulting from the doctrine of responsibility held by the Chinese Government was often severely felt. In 1782, a ship supposed to be Spanish property, and to have a Dutch cargo on board, bound from Macao to Manilla, was seized by Captain M'Lary, commanding a country ship from Bengal. The Governor of Macao, in the first instance, resented this infraction of the neutrality of his port, by imprisoning the aggressor, and fining him to the amount of 70,000 dollars. But when the circumstance came to be known to the Mandarins at Canton, the Company's supercargoes were informed that they would be considered as answerable for the restoration of the ship in that instance, and in future for any similar transgression. The abandonment of the captured vessel by M'Lary and his crew, happily prevented any attempt to give effect to the menace.

In 1784, a Chinese was accidentally killed by a shot fired from on board the Lady Hughes country ship, in the act of saluting, the consequence of which was the execution of the gunner. Apprehensions being entertained by the Company's representatives, that the vessel which occasioned the unlucky accident, might slip out of the river before the affair was investigated, they were compelled, with a view to their own security, so far to exceed their powers, as to order the commanders of the Company's ships to prevent her sailing; and when the fate of the unfortunate gunner was ultimately decided, a deputation from all the European factories was summoned to attend the Mandarin of Justice, who acquainted its members distinctly and unequivocally, that on any similar occasion that might thereafter occur, if the actual offender could not be found, the chiefs of their respective nations should be considered as answerable in their own persons.

Another occurrence took place in the same or following season, which shewed that the Chinese Government consider the Chief of the Company's factory as responsible not only for the peaceable conduct of his countrymen, but for their pecuniary engagements. Some difference in the settlement of an account having arisen between the commander of a country ship and his *security merchant*, (a term which will be afterwards explained) the latter had withheld the grand chop or port clearance, without which no pilot would take charge of the ship. The master confiding in his own skill, resolved to remove his ship without one. In this predicament the Chinese neither attempted by force to stop the ship, nor molested the person of the commander, but conformably to their usual practice, had recourse to the Company's representatives, threatening them with a suspension of their trade, if the ship was suffered to proceed to sea before the difference was adjusted; on which the Company's supercargoes again interfered, (although unauthorized) to prevent the sailing of the ship.

Farther, it was owing to the excesses and unwarrantable speculations entered into by some unlicensed British traders, who contracted large debts, which they were unable to pay, that the prices of Chinese commodities were increased to the Company in 1780 by the Hong merchants. In order to establish a fund for the liquidation of those debts, the prices of tea and other exports were then raised to a standard from which they have never since been lowered; and had the effect been foreseen, it might have been wise as a measure of œconomy, for the Company to avert it, by paying the debts at once, out of their own treasury.

In consequence of the occurrences above adverted to, and others of a similar nature, the Court of Directors, perceiving, that from the maxims of responsibility laid down and promulgated by the Chinese Government, their best interests were liable to injury from the folly, rashness, or dishonesty of individuals, became impressed with the necessity of investing their representatives with some legal power of control. They accordingly issued orders to all their Presidencies in India that no ship should be allowed to clear out from thence to China until the captain and owners had entered into an engagement, under a certain penalty, to conform implicitly to such regulations as the Company's supercargoes should think proper to enact for their guidance during their stay on the Chinese coast, and the captains were required to present certificates of their clearances to the head of the Company's factory immediately on their arrival at Canton.

The commutation act having passed soon after, the consequent increase both of the Company's and country shipping, pointed out the expediency of some more efficient regulations than had hitherto existed for restraining the disorderly behaviour of the seamen; and a species of police was instituted, under the superintendence of the senior commander of the Company's ships, to which all British ships frequenting Canton are now subject. Many good effects have unquestionably been produced by these regulations, but when the difficulties arising from the peculiar character of the Chinese on the one hand, and the rash, impetuous, and dissolute character of our sailors on the other, are considered, it is perhaps matter of greater surprise, that the intercourse has been preserved at all, than that it has been liable to casual interruption.

Chinese women are strictly prohibited by the laws of the empire from going on board of foreign ships. The consequences of such an offence, though difficult of prevention, are very serious. In 1801, a country ship, called the Dove, was detained several weeks in the river on this account, to the injury of the owners and all concerned.

A man committing an outrage in a state of intoxication, according to the criminal code of China, is exiled to a desert country, there to remain in servitude.

By the same laws, the abetting, or encouraging of emigration, is punished as a capital crime. It would be absurd to suppose that violations of such laws do not under present circumstances frequently occur. Indeed the loss of men on board the Company's ships, from casualties, desertion, or the impress for His Majesty's service, often makes it indispensably necessary to engage a certain number of Chinese seamen for the homeward voyage, because the ships could not be otherwise navigated. But the vigilance exercised by the Company's officers, renders some of these offences more rare; their local knowledge renders others less easy of detection, and the influence possessed by their Supercargoes, as a body, on all occasions secures to their representations a more favourable hearing from the government, than those of individuals could be expected to obtain.

Notwithstanding these various advantages, however, occurrences have happened even of late years, arising out of the severity of the Chinese laws respecting homicide, which have been productive of much inconvenience and embarrassment, and threatened a total extinction of the trade. In 1807, a Chinese died in consequence of a wound which he had received in an affray with part of the crew belonging to one of the Company's ships. An order was immediately issued by the government at Canton, to deliver up the guilty person, and in the mean time an entire stop was put to the trade. An investigation was instituted by the commander of the suspected ship, for the discovery of the culprit, but without effect. The inquiry was farther pursued by the Chinese Mandarins themselves, and with no better success. An individual was indeed selected as one of the most active in the affray, but the guilt of inflicting the wound that had proved fatal, was not brought home to him. At last, after much discussion, an anxious interval of six weeks, and considerable expense incurred by demurrage, the ships were permitted to depart; but in consequence of this delay, the whole China fleet were obliged, under many disadvantages, to return to Europe by the Eastward passage, instead of the usual course. In 1810 and 1811, the trade met with another obstruction from a similar cause.

In mentioning these circumstances, it is due to the Company's representatives at Canton, at the same time to state, that the difficulties to which they have been on various occasions subjected, have uniformly been surmounted by good sense, firmness, and moderation; and that, notwithstanding the jeopardy into which their persons, their property, and the interests of their employers, have been repeatedly thrown by unavoidable accident, they never have sacrificed the life or freedom of one of His Majesty's subjects to their own safety or extrication from embarrassment. Can it be believed by any one, that private individuals under like circumstances, would have been equally scrupulous and equally successful?

The principle of responsibility maintained and acted upon by the Chinese Government, in regard to strangers (as already explained), has been acknowledged by the Company in their regulations, and is, of course, confirmed by that recognition. They had, in fact, no other alternative than either to abandon the trade altogether, or to carry it on conformably to the laws and usages of China. It was equally beyond the Company's power to change the nature, or to resist the operation of the Chinese Institutions, unprotected as they have been by any existing treaty, and unsupported by the influence of a resident British Ambassador. Is it not then most unreasonable to expect that the Company should extend their protection to their rivals in trade; and would it not be unjust to permit the private merchants of this country to place themselves in a situation in which experience has shewn that their errors, their faults, and their crimes would be exclusively visited on the Company? Were private British merchants admitted to a participation of the trade, it would be useless for the Company to disclaim all authority over them. As long as an English flag continues to fly at Canton, the Chinese will never be persuaded that every ship bearing the same colours with the Company's ships, ought not to be subject to the control of the Company's agents. An inevitable consequence of the trade being thrown open is, that the ships of individual merchants would claim the protection of the Company's supercargoes whenever they involved themselves in difficulty, and would spurn their control when they found constraint inconvenient or unpleasant.

Another obstacle to a free trade presents itself: When the Chinese first entered into commercial intercourse with other countries, their cautious and wary Government, with a view to avoid all cause of dispute or quarrel, constituted a certain number of native merchants into a body for the management of foreign trade, and at the same time, that it imposed an interdict against every trader who had not one of its own subjects as his security, it left the option of becoming or refusing to become security to each individual composing this body of native merchants. *The security merchants* being answerable to their own Government for every act of those for whom security is given, are thus subjected to a heavy responsibility, and though they may have little scruple about being guarantees for the Company's agents, after the long experience they have had of their probity and discretion, they would probably hesitate before committing themselves for the conduct of a motley class of new adventurers, in whom they could repose no such confidence.

Were a representative of the British Government appointed to the station now filled by the agents of the Company, and also to be recognized in that capacity by the Emperor of China (by no means a matter of course), it is worth consideration, setting aside the expense to the public, whether such a representative, without force to carry his orders into execution, would be adequate to the end of his appointment; whether any representative with such a force could be expected placidly to submit to the indignities to which he might occasionally be exposed; and whether a change of system might not infuse such distrust both into the Chinese Government and the security merchants as to produce a suspension of the trade, or occasion such differences as might eventually lead to our total exclusion from their ports? The existence of the trade would unquestionably be endangered by relaxing the controling power, under which it is now carried on; and this relaxation could hardly fail to result either from changing the hands in which the power is at present vested, or from extending the sphere of its operation, so far as to render superintendence difficult if not impracticable.

Among the evils that would arise from throwing open the trade between England and China, that of smuggling articles of British manufacture into the Chinese territories in contravention of the revenue laws of the empire, is one which might with certainty be anticipated. Individuals engaged in separate adventures would naturally endeavour to promote their immediate interests, little scrupulous about the means. The evasion of the duties on woollens, which on some articles are equal to 60 and 70 per cent. on the sale prices, and considerable on all, would prove an irresistible temptation to fraud; and though it is impossible accurately to predict the consequences of such an abuse, it seems no unnatural or overstretched conclusion, that a government, jealous of its rights, and distinguished by a singular antipathy to strangers, might thereby be induced to break off all commercial intercourse with a country, when that intercourse ceased to be conducted on the principles of honesty and fair dealing. The East India Company, as a body, stand far above the suspicion of lending themselves to practices of such a nature, and every attention is paid to prevent them on the part of the officers employed in the Company's ships. The Court of Directors have very properly issued orders, that any officer detected in smuggling goods into China, shall be deprived of his portion of tonnage for a home investment, and this regulation has been found much more effectual in preventing illicit traffic, than the fine of fifty times the value of the smuggled article, to which the offender is subject in case of detection by the Chinese laws.

It will probably be asked, do not the Americans carry on an open trade with China successfully, and might not private British merchants do the same?— To this question it may be replied, that the dispositions and habits of the seamen employed by the two countries are materially different, and that the political circumstances of the two countries themselves, have by no means, of late years, been so nearly analogous, as to warrant a fair comparison between their respective gains from the trade. The American seamen are, generally speaking, a sedate, orderly, and regular class of people. Particular care also is taken in selecting those who are employed to man their China ships. Where no competition of demand exists between the government and the merchants, this selection is always easy, and the large profits in trade which the American merchants have made in consequence of their access to foreign ports, from which Great Britain is excluded, enable them to offer to their seamen very high wages, so high as thirty dollars, or £7. per month, and not unfrequently a share in the adventure. A common American sailor may look forward, by a course of good behaviour, to become mate, or even master of a ship. Nothing can be more unpleasant than to say any thing to the disparagement of a body of men to whom this country is so eminently indebted, but it is well known that the British seamen, particularly such as in time of war compose the crews of trading ships, do not answer precisely the above description. Dauntless in the midst of danger, bold in battle, and easily restrained on board of King's ships, but insubordinate in the merchant service, addicted to liquor, and prone to every excess when on shore, even under the eye of their own officers, it becomes quite impossible to ensure their good behaviour at a foreign port, particularly after a long voyage. The exigencies of the navy during a period of hostility, leave only the gleanings and refuse of the profession to the trade. The natural and habitual turbulence of such men, it has required all the vigilance and energy of the Company's representatives at Canton to control. The existing checks have not always been found sufficient to repress disorder, and were they either set aside or weakened, the total exclusion of our ships from the ports and rivers of China would be a consummation to be deprecated indeed, but not easily to be averted.

If the petitioners for an open trade found their claims upon an assumption, that the great profits made by the Americans upon *their* share of it could either be participated or engrossed by the rival exertions of private British merchants, they state and argue upon a fallacy. The gains of the Americans, if they exist to the extent supposed, are chiefly to be ascribed to the pacific policy of their government, and to the commercial relations in which they stand, or have stood, with the rest of the world. It may be asserted, without fear of contradiction, that in the event either of a general peace, or of the continuance of war between Great Britain and the United States, America cannot maintain a successful competition with the East India Company in the China trade.—The woollens and metals exported from England by the Company, and the cotton, sandal wood, pepper, and other commodities exported to China from the British territories in India, by the Company, and by the Chinese themselves, are now sufficient in value to pay the whole of the Company's home investment from China. The Americans carry little thither besides silver, and therefore their gains must be confined to the profits on their return cargoes; whereas the Company have a mercantile profit upon *a large proportion* of their imports to China, and a profit upon the whole of their exports from that country.—Their gains in the trade would be still more extensive, but the produce and manufactures of this country, which they export to China, are selected less with a view to mercantile profit than to the encouragement of British industry, by procuring a vent for our own commodities. It must be obvious to every one that the general profits of the Company are much diminished by the advance of taxation, by war freights, war insurance, and the necessity imposed upon them by a state of hostility, of sending their ships out and home in fleets, and under convoy. It should, however, at the same time be recollected, that private British merchants would be subjected (were the trade thrown open) to precisely the same inconveniences and drawbacks.

The inference which the foregoing facts and observations seem to justify, is, that the present mode of conducting the trade between England and China could not be changed without endangering the suspension, or perhaps, the total suppression of the existing intercourse; and this consideration alone is of sufficient weight to counterbalance the pretensions of those whose object it is to invade the exclusive privilege of the East India Company. It will not however be difficult to shew that the manufactures of this country, the government itself, and the great body of British consumers are as much interested in the continuance of the Company's exclusive privilege as that Corporation itself. This constitutes the

2d Branch of the subject to which it was proposed to draw the reader's attention.

The two principal articles of British produce and manufacture exported by the East India Company to China, are tin and woollens. It appears from the Printed Papers,* that in consequence of an arrangement entered into between the Company and certain proprietors of tin mines, in the County of Cornwall, in 1789, an average annual quantity of 756 tons of that metal, at the average prime cost of £74. 1s.

* Page 88.

per ton, has been exported to China in the course of the 22 years subsequent to that agreement; that no charge has been made by the Company for freight, trouble, and expense incurred in England in shipping the tin; that after allowing 4½ per cent. for insurance, 2 per cent. for commission and charges in China, and four months' interest for advance of money, the tin actually costs the Company £80. per ton—and that the average sale price in China has been £84. per ton, leaving to the Company a difference in their receipts beyond their disbursements of only £3. 18*s.* as a compensation for freight and charges of establishment. It farther appears, that in the present season the Court of Directors agreed to receive 800 tons, at the advanced price of £78. per ton, by which, according to the same calculation, the Company will actually incur a loss of 7*s.* 4*d.* per ton, exclusive of freight and charges of insurance. The sacrifice made by the Company for the encouragement of the tin miners may be duly appreciated, by referring to the same letter, where the Chairman and Deputy state,* that at Malacca, Banca, and other places in the Eastern parts of India, they could procure tin at from £67. to £70. a ton, (and *that* probably in exchange for the productions of our Indian territories); at which price the sales in the China market would leave them a fair mercantile profit upon this branch of their trade.

* Printed Papers, page 89.

In so far therefore as the proprietors of tin mines are interested in the pending discussion, the opening of the trade to China would be injurious to them, it being obviously unreasonable to expect that individual merchants would make the same sacrifices that the Company have made, and seem still willing to continue, for the purpose of procuring a vent for one of the staple productions of the British soil.

Another no less certain effect of throwing open the trade, would be a great reduction in the export of British woollens. The introduction of woollen manufactures into China, is of recent date, and the exports of that article, which, at the commencement of the trade, amounted in value only to a few thousand pounds, has been progressively augmented by the exertions and sacrifices of the East India Company, to near a million sterling annually. The French and Dutch attempted to introduce the woollen manufactures of their respective countries into China, but with very little success.—The Americans have occasionally, though very rarely, carried woollens to Canton, but the adventures, not having turned out profitable in a single instance, were never repeated by the same individuals. Although the commodity is peculiarly well adapted to the climate of the northern provinces of the Chinese empire, the inhabitants, provided with a substitute in furs of various descriptions, to which they have been long accustomed, have been found averse to a dress exceeding in price, but inferior in durability to their usual clothing, harsher in its texture than their own cottons and silks, and less warm than their coverings of skins. Articles similar to the poplins and tabbinets of Ireland, are manufactured in China in abundance, and at a much cheaper rate than Ireland can afford to furnish them. The records of the East India Company not only afford ample evidence of the difficulties attending the sale of the woollens which they export, but also exhibit a series of very heavy losses sustained in this branch of the trade, although the confidence reposed by the Chinese in the honesty and good faith of the Company's agents is such, that a bale of goods passes from one province of the empire to another, and through a vast number of different hands, merely upon the credit of the Company's seal, without ever being examined, just as their merchandise imported into this country, and bought at their sales, used to pass upon the credit of the same sign over the whole continent of Europe. Notwithstanding this advantage, however, which new adventurers would not possess, the Company have lost nearly £50,000 a year, in the course of their present charter, on the article of long ells alone, imported into China, though only 10 per cent has been added in their accounts to the prime cost, to form the invoice price of the goods, and to cover all charges of freight, insurance, interest for money advanced, &c.; the goods being regularly paid for to the manufacturer in ready money, and sometimes a year and a half before the value is realized in China. The motives for continuing a trade so disadvantageous, are understood to be founded on the following considerations: that it became the Company to incur a temporary loss for the sake of great public objects;—that had they exclusively consulted their own interests as a commercial body, thousands of British manufacturers who have been supported by their capital must have been reduced to distress and ruin; that the present unhappy state of the world ought not to be contemplated as permanent; that the stagnation of trade resulting from events of a transitory nature was to be counteracted by their corporate exertions in opening and even forcing outlets to the staple manufactures of this country, wherever such outlets could be found; that these exertions have hitherto hindered a temporary check to British industry from proving the cause of its lasting decline; that their exports of commodities have prevented the alternative of an addition to the heavy existing drain of specie from Great Britain, or a defalcation in the revenue, which must have ensued from a diminished importation of tea from China; and, that the loss incurred by the Company from this mode of carrying on the trade, has been in fact a part of the price paid to the public for the continuance of their exclusive privileges. Whether these considerations will be satisfactory to the political economist may be doubted: still the motives of the Company are entitled at least to indulgence, and if in circumstances where they had only a choice of evils, they have yielded to what appeared to them to be the least injurious, they have established a claim upon the gratitude of the country instead of meriting attack. If they have erred, it has been in common with the manufacturing capitalists of Manchester, Birmingham, and other towns in the kingdom, who have continued to retain their workmen in their employ after their labour ceased to be valuable.* The reign of general principles has long since passed away, or rather has not yet commenced in the world. Man is the creature of expedient, and compromise is the law of his condition. If, forsaking the course that has been traced to us by experience, we are to tempt the region of untried speculation, we may begin with tearing every commercial treaty from the archives of the state, and committing half of our statutes to the flames.

---

* See evidence taken in a Committee of the House of Commons on the Orders in Council, passim.

The Edinburgh Reviewers in commenting upon this evidence observe: "It is pleasing, indeed, and consolatory in the midst "of such a scene as is disclosed by the evidence before us, to see "in how many instances the latter description of persons (the "capitalist, the merchant, and the master manufacturers of all "degrees) continued to give employment to their workmen, long "after they ceased to make any profit by their labours; and even "went on for a great length of time to maintain them at a loss to "themselves. There is no national distinction so honourable, as "that of breeding a race of men among whom such conduct con-"fers no distinction." *Edinburgh Review*, No. XXXIX. p. 235.

Admitting the accuracy of the facts which have been stated, the following inferences will hardly be disputed.

1st. That the demand for British produce and manufactures in China being extremely limited, and supplied by the East India Company as exporters at a loss, the gains of the producers and manufacturers must necessarily cease, or be diminished, in the same proportion with the sacrifices of the Company, and that these sacrifices cannot be expected either on the part of that body, or of individuals after the opening of the trade, inasmuch as the Company will then be unable, and individuals will both be unable and unwilling to continue them. If the credit of the articles now exported were shaken in such an empire as China, it is impossible to say what might be the permanent effects to the manufacturers at home; and even a temporary derangement in the export of one of the great staples of the country, could not fail to occasion much distress and clamour.

2dly. That the merchants are soliciting admission not to a profitable but to a losing commerce, in so far as the *export* trade to China is concerned, and that if capital be embarked in it, it must necessarily prove ruinous to the speculators: and

3dly. That the Legislature will best provide for the true interest of the various classes placed under its protecting care and superintendence, by attending to facts rather than to speculation, by listening to experience rather than to vague expectations, and by refusing to hazard known, certain, and permanent advantages for a chance of something better, coupled with the numerous causes and lamentable consequences of miscarriage.

The claimants of an open trade will, no doubt, urge, that though the *export* branch of it may be unprofitable, yet that the commerce *upon the whole* must be advantageous, and that they are entitled to share in the advantage to its full extent. In order fairly to appreciate the merits of this pretension, it is necessary to consider what would be its probable operation, if sanctioned by the Legislature, upon the Revenue, and the general interests of this Country.

As to the question of *natural right*, on which the claim is founded, in some of the Petitions, it is to be observed, that on the first establishment of society, the rights of individuals are merged in the interests of the community at large, and that it is incumbent upon Government, the legitimate guardian of those interests, to protect them no less against private encroachment, than against foreign aggression. There are, in fact, no other natural rights in society than what are recognized by the *Laws* of Society. Commercial freedom, taken in the abstract, is quite as desirable as political freedom: but every person who is in the habit of attending to the numerous statutes connected with trade and revenue, which at different periods have been passed by the Legislature, must be aware that the principle of liberty, as applied to commerce, is so modified and variously restricted, as hardly to be recognized in the system under which the commerce of the country is now carried on. To promote demand, and to facilitate supply, ought to be the great object of all commercial policy; but the tendency of the whole of our navigation laws, is to render the produce of our own soil and industry less accessible to foreigners, and to enhance the price of foreign productions to the British consumer. By appropriating to ourselves a monopoly (under certain limitations) of the trade, between the parent state and the colonies, we stinted colonial, and taxed domestic industry; and by attempting to engross a large proportion of the carrying trade between this and other countries, we paid in the increase of price for the articles imported, a sum far exceeding both our gains and savings, under the different heads of freight, insurance and commission. These laws were passed at a period when political security was justly deemed of paramount importance to the commercial freedom, which they invaded; and though in later times, when from the pressure of war, and the general circumstances of the world, our commerce is considered as being more in danger than our power, it has been deemed advisable to act upon a contrary maxim, and not only to relax the navigation act, but to permit the trade of the country to be carried on, at least in part, through the medium of alien enemies (a maxim fully as hazardous to our political ascendency as that which it supplanted, had been injurious to our commercial prosperity), the change is universally regarded, not as the effect of a free and enlightened choice, nor as a homage paid to the principle of commercial freedom, but as a tribute extorted by necessity, and limited by the extent and duration of that necessity. So impossible is it frequently to reconcile in practice principles in themselves equally true, and so vain is it to attempt, under all circumstances, to pursue an uniform and invariable line of conduct deducible from any one fixed principle!

It would not be difficult to shew that the *spirit* of monopoly, (whatever odium may be attached to the *term*), is not so abhorrent either to the Municipal Institutions or Statute Laws of this Country, as the arguments and pretensions of the adversaries of the East India Company might lead one to suppose.—What are all the Corporations now existing in the Kingdom, founded upon ancient Charters, and fortified by separate codes of by-laws, but so many legal monopolies, each not only exercising jurisdiction over its own members, but prescribing terms of admission to such persons as may wish to pursue any branch of trade within its limits, and proportioning the fine of entrance to the local advantages of the situation? If *natural right* is to be appealed to, why should the City of London, for instance, possess the power of excluding from the exercise of trade within its bounds, every man in the country who has not served an apprenticeship to one of its affiliated members, or who is unable to pay the usual price for a share in their immunities? Nay, why are apprenticeships thought necessary at all, and why might not success and failure be left as a test of qualification for business, in the same way that demand in the market, and discrimination in the purchasers, are allowed to regulate the value of other commodities? Or, why should the College of Physicians possess the sole power (which no medical practitioner can invade with impunity) of treating all diseases within the precincts of the metropolis? Upon this principle, charters, indentures, and diplomas, must be considered unjust and useless usurpations upon the common rights of mankind. The Poor Laws, operating equally with Corporations, as an obstruction to the free circulation of industry, ought also to be abolished.—The Church Establishment itself, the Universities, and the various foundations of scholarships, and exhibitions connected with them, interfering, as they do, with the regular distribution of industry and stock, and introducing an unnatural competition into certain pursuits, must, in like manner, give way to the sweep of innovation. If the principle that is contended for shall be assumed as the foundation of a practical rule of conduct, what is to become of all the laws establishing and fencing the monopoly held by the woollen manufacturers of this country? The strict prohibitions against the export of wool, in its raw state, the duties imposed on Scotch and Irish linens, when used for home consumption, and the bounties granted on their exportation, are so many encouragements held out by the Legislature, to the woollen manufacturers, at the expense not only of other classes of artisans, but of the landed proprietors, and the consumers of animal food, soap, candles, and other necessaries of life, and it has also been often alleged that they serve to the deterioration of the quality of our wool. The difference again in the rates of duties levied on sugars of West India and East India growth, is founded on a preference, advantageous indeed to the colonial trade, but disadvantageous in the same proportion to the East India Company, the Asiatic planter, and the British consumer.

It would be easy, likewise, to demonstrate, that the arguments which are adduced in support of complete liberty of commerce, among all the individuals of a state, might with equal propriety, and equal force, be urged in favour of the same liberty of commerce between one state and another, and that the whole international policy of Europe, as exhibited in commercial treaties, as well as municipal laws, has been at variance with what are called the established maxims of political economy. There is more than plausibility in the doctrine, that a nation, instead of necessarily thriving by the ruin of its neighbour, ultimately suffers from the decline of its commercial rival; that the prosperity of any single country must spread to the several countries lying within the sphere of its intercourse, till the productions of each are common to all, or till riches cease to beget wants, and wants to require gratification. A general monopoly of trade, therefore, were it attainable, would eventually prove injurious to the country possessing it, because a surplus stock of productions, without a market, contributes no more to wealth than if the commodities had never existed, and because a market presupposes not only want and supply, but the presence of *money*, or some *other medium of exchange*, the scarcity, or abundance, of which will be in an exact ratio to the of means obtaining it, or, in other words, to the proportion of trade which has eluded the grasp of the monopoly. Beautiful as this theory is, when fully developed, not only for its abstract truth, but its tendency to illustrate the beneficent designs of Providence in regard to man, yet, it has never been acted upon, and must remain impracticable, until passion has abdicated her empire, and reason assumed her rightful sway in the affairs of the world. To live in peace, and minister to each other's comfort, was the object and law of our creation, and had we fulfilled our original destiny, many fair and comely theories might have been realized, which now only play in delightful vision before our fancies. Since war became part of our occupation, to provide for its wants, has been a necessary object of our policy, and an irregular ambition has infused itself into all our aims. Hence we have been driven from unerring principles to loose expedients; and how much soever the effect may be lamented, remedy is hopeless, while the cause continues to operate.

Without going into farther detail, for the purpose of exposing those pretensions which professedly rest upon natural right, and abstract fitness, and which are not more incompatible with the exclusive privileges of the East India Company, than with the whole policy of our commercial system, and the actual state of human affairs; it is of more importance to examine the practical advantages which result to the Country, from the privileges hitherto conferred on the Company, and the probable consequences of a refusal on the part of the Legislature to renew those privileges.

The tea imported from China by the Company, pays to Government an annual net revenue of about £3,500,000., varying little from year to year, and collected with hardly any expense to the public. The saving thus effected under the head of collection alone (supposing the average charge of realizing the public revenue to be 5 per cent.) amounts to £175,000. per annum; and the influence of the Crown is diminished to the same extent in which the saving takes place: a consideration which it may be presumed will have no small weight with those whose constitutional jealousy sees the growth of that influence, in the increase of taxation. The duties upon tea in every view in which they can be considered, may be regarded as constituting one of the least exceptionable and most valuable sources of revenue.—Without being an indispensable necessary of life, the article is one of universal use; the tax, therefore, is exempt from all the disadvantages of imposts upon necessaries, and is at the same time far more productive than the most of those which are levied upon luxuries. It is optional with every person to pay it or not, and to pay it at what times, and in what proportions he may find convenient. Being levied upon consumption, and graduated according to the different qualities of the commodity consumed, it is not only equal in its operation, but accommodates itself to the means of the consumers. Neither the supply nor the demand depending upon the varying relations of European States, the revenue derived from tea is certain, and free from those fluctuations to which the produce of many other taxes is liable. Unlike spirits, which though productive to Government, are injurious to the health and morals of the people, the beverage is not only harmless in itself, but is the source of much innocent enjoyment. The solace of the weary, and the cordial of the sick, the enlivener of gaiety, and the soother of care, it ministers to the comfort of the cottage, and the delight of the palace, uniting the rich and the poor, and the sexes together by a bland assimilation of habit.

The importance of so large a revenue derived from a source so unobjectionable, must be generally felt and acknowledged; and if its security be incompatible with the pretensions of the claimants of an open trade, the smaller object ought certainly to give way to the greater.

The temptation to smuggling, held out by the chance of evading the duty, (amounting on tea, to 96 per cent.), is such as no legal penalties could counteract, were private merchants admitted into the trade; and in the event of its being opened to the outports, the opportunities of fraud would be so multiplied, as to defy the utmost vigilance of the largest possible establishment of revenue officers.— Individual integrity has been at all times found to afford a very feeble security for the realization of national revenue, and though there be no moral distinction between an act of public and private dishonesty, it is well known that many persons who revolt at the idea of taking an unfair advantage of their neighbours, do not hesitate to defraud Government of its dues. The character of the East India Company as a body, their responsibility to, and dependence on the Legislature, together with the control they possess over their servants, constitute a guarantee for the fairness and regularity of their transactions, which private merchants could not furnish either individually or as a class. The Company's ships arrive periodically in fleets, their imports are brought to one place, lodged under the keys of the Government officers, and sold in presence of those officers, who have no farther trouble than to ascertain the amount of the duties, which are carefully levied, and punctually paid by the Company.—A system at once so safe, and so little expensive with a view to the collection of revenue, it is impossible for human ingenuity to devise, and any attempt to supersede it, must be attended with a great addition to the public charge, and a considerable increase of patronage to Government, while in the end, it will be found utterly ineffectual for the object which it has in view. A short time ago a ship was discovered in the river smuggling tea, purchased from an American at Gibraltar, part of the cargo having been previously landed in the Channel, and on the western coast of the kingdom, without detection. On the return of peace, the only effectual mode of preventing the introduction of smuggled tea from the Continent, will probably be a reduction of the existing duties. In time of war, such a sacrifice of revenue would certainly be attended with great inconvenience, and yet the measure of laying open the trade now contended for, would introduce that state of things during war, which would necessarily require either a voluntary relinquishment on the part of Government, of a portion of the present duties, or give rise to that evasion of them which is only to be apprehended on a return of peace.

The smuggling of tea would be productive of the double mischief of disabling the East India Company from paying the dividends upon their stock, and of compelling the Government to have recourse to other sources of revenue, in consequence of a defalcation of the duties on that article; and is it supposable that the Legislature, admitting that there was no other danger in the experiment, would put to hazard the credit of the first corporation in the world, and the stability of three millions and a half of annual revenue, in order not to open new channels of prosperity and national wealth, but merely to transfer a portion of that trade to individuals which has hitherto been exclusively carried on by the East India Company? This is a question affecting not solely the parties immediately concerned in the pending discussion; it is one in which every individual in the Country has a direct interest. If a considerable deficiency in the revenue takes place, are the claimants of an open trade either able or willing to make it good? Must it not, on the contrary, be supplied by means of general taxation, and in the present burdened state of the nation, it will be readily admitted that it is much easier to devise and assess new taxes than to collect them. But regulations, it seems, are to be framed so as to guard against the danger of an illicit trade, and to protect the Company and the revenue from its effects.* It is to be observed, however, that these regulations do not contemplate any infringement upon the Company's exclusive privilege to the *China* trade. Their object is solely to prevent an illicit trade in *India* commodities, in the event of the trade with India being opened to the Out-ports; and whoever has read with attention and impartiality the letters of the Deputation of the Court of Directors to the President of the Board of Commissioners of the 15th and 29th April, 1812,† will more than doubt the efficacy of such regulations, (however strong they may be) even for the limited purpose which they are said to have in view. The regulation most obviously necessary, certainly, is a strict prohibition of the importation into this country of the produce of China in any but the Company's ships, as without this prohibition the continuance of their exclusive privilege would be merely nominal, and the idea of protecting either their interests, or those of the revenue, would be altogether chimerical. The facility with which cargoes of tea might be procured at Java and the other islands in the Indian seas, would completely defeat the views, both of the Company and the Government. During the American war the Dutch were supplied at Batavia with tea carried thither by Chinese junks, at a cheaper rate than it could

* Printed Papers, p. 148. † Pages 108 and 148.

have been provided at Canton. The teas received at that emporium are brought from the central provinces of the empire by inland navigation, frequently interrupted by land carriage over mountainous tracts, at an expense far exceeding the freight to Batavia from the ports of China contiguous to the tea country. The cost of inland conveyance, the profit of the Hong merchants, and the charges and extortions with which the trade is loaded at Canton, may fairly be estimated at 33 per cent. upon the original value of the tea. It is easy to perceive therefore, that the Company could not withstand a competition of this sort, and that the revenue, if an intermediate trade were permitted, would be exposed to the same danger that it would encounter, upon the trade being thrown entirely open.

These remarks naturally lead to a consideration of the principal question on which the parties interested are now at issue.

It appears from the Papers which have been printed, respecting the Negociation between His Majesty's Ministers and the Court of Directors, for a renewal of the East India Company's exclusive Privileges, that a difference of sentiment (perhaps an irreconcilable one) exists between the Government of the country and the Representatives of the Company, upon the expediency of confining the Trade with India to the Port of London, or of opening it to the Out-ports, and that in consequence of neither party being convinced by the arguments advanced by the other, in support of their opposite opinions, the Negociation experienced a temporary suspension, and the deliberations in Parliament upon the merits of the Company's Petition were unexpectedly deferred from the last to the next Session.—The delay, in one view, can hardly fail to excite regret. In proportion as the period draws near at which the term of the Company's present Charter expires, the urgency of a Legislative decision upon the question of renewing it, or of substituting another arrangement for the administration of the British territories in India, and for the conduct of the trade between Great Britain and Asia becomes exceedingly pressing. Uncertainty regarding the duration of a Government, tends both to diminish its authority and to relax its exertions; and the mere commercial concerns of the East India Company are of such magnitude as to require a much longer period than two years to wind up. The opportunity, on the other hand, which the delay would afford for inquiry and reflection, presents some equivalent advantage for these inconveniences: an advantage which certainly will not be under-rated by those who think that already too much has been yielded to ill-founded prejudice and popular clamour, and who expect from sober investigation, modified demands rather than farther concessions.

If the Directors of the East India Company entertain

any respect for the opinions of the Statesman who long presided over the administration of their affairs, or if they are disposed to listen with reverence to his solemn and almost parting counsel, it will be impossible for them ever to agree to the extension of the trade with India to the Out-ports, against which that able Minister so recently cautioned them in terms the most direct and pointed.* Let it be remembered that the advice referred to, was tendered for the purpose of dissuading the Company from interfering in the appointment of agents for the private trade in India, farther than by license; and the ground on which it was given was, that supposing the principle then inculcated was observed, (viz. that the trade continued to be carried on under a monopoly, as limited by the act of 1793, and subject to such ulterior modifications as circumstances might suggest without doing violence to the system)—the Company would find a sufficient *commercial* security against an abuse of the privileges which it was then proposed, or which it might afterwards be deemed expedient to grant, in the existing provision that no goods should be imported from India that were not deposited in their warehouses and disposed of at their sales. Against any infringement of this provision, the late Lord Melville (then Mr. Dundas) at the same time warned them that it

---

* See Mr. Dundas's Letter of the 2d of April, 1800, as quoted page 41.

was *their great interest to guard*, and could he have foreseen, not only that his principle would be abandoned (as it *virtually* now is), but that the Company would be called upon to give up the only security they possess against a fraudulent invasion of their trade, his Letter would have been more appropriately couched in terms of condolence than of admonition.

The general objections, against a change of system, have more or less weight according to the extent of change which may be in contemplation; and the efficacy of those safeguards, which may be proposed for the protection of the revenue and higher objects, will very much depend upon the difficulty of either violating or eluding their operation. It is the nature of all restrictive regulations, to lose in force what they gain in expansion. The *principle* is not yet *avowed*, for example, of permitting the unlimited ingress of Europeans into our Indian territories. But if ships are allowed to clear out indiscriminately from all the ports of the United Kingdom for India, it will be impossible, under any system of precautions, to prevent the evil which all seem desirous to avert; and it would be no less unreasonable than impolitic to place the East India Company in a situation in which they would be held responsible for the tranquillity and good government of our Asiatic possessions, while, at the same time, they were precluded from the exercise of that control at home which is indispensably necessary to the maintenance of their authority abroad. As well might they, in the event of the import trade from India being opened to the British Out-ports, be made answerable for the loss which the revenue would inevitably sustain from the fraudulent practices of individuals with whom they were in no way connected, as for the conduct of persons in India who went thither in defiance of legislative prohibitions. The Governments at the different Presidencies indeed might, as they no doubt would, be invested with power not only to restrain, but to send home unlicensed adventurers; but it cannot escape attention, that almost all the odium attending the exercise of that power would ultimately fall upon the Court of Directors, and that the unpopularity of the Government at home, would be in exact proportion to the vigilance and energy displayed by the delegated authorities in India. There would be no end to complaints, petitions, and remonstrances. Failure in adventures would be felt as a grievance, imputed misconduct represented as a cloak and excuse for oppression, and limited privilege treated as a mockery of unlimited right. The press would teem with the narratives of the discontented, and in the absence of other redress, *invective* would be resorted to by the sufferers, as a plentiful source of consolation. However much some men may affect to despise attacks of this sort, it certainly is not wise to provoke, and far less to make deliberative provision for them. Those, on the other hand, who are disposed to make a partial surrender of their own judgment to popular prejudice, should at least bear in mind that they may on a future occasion be called on to complete the sacrifice, and that the clamour might be more easily resisted now than after it shall have been strengthened by initiation, and embittered by disappointment in the trade. Commercial speculations are not of a nature to admit of persons embarking in them one year, and withdrawing from them the next, or as soon as they are found not to answer expectation. The merchant cannot change the theatre of his transactions as he can the place of his abode. When capital is engaged, credit established, and connexion formed, he has seldom any alternative but to persevere, or become bankrupt. But in the case supposed, he would have a *tertium quid* in his option, namely, to arraign the system of government; and to this expedient he would unquestionably have recourse without minutely calculating whether his efforts to subvert it would prove fruitless or successful. The last consideration well merits attention before *any infringement* of the East India Company's existing privileges (modified as the exercise of them has been by the voluntary admission of a number of respectable individuals into the India trade) shall be definitively resolved upon. But were there no other objection to the extreme concession of *allowing ships to sail from the Out-ports of this Country*, the facility which it would afford to persons of improper characters and sinister views, of getting clandestinely to India, seems on all pruden-tial grounds to interpose an insuperable obstacle in the way of its adoption. It is hardly necessary to observe, that if no ships were permitted to clear out for India, excepting from the port of London, the facility alluded to would be very much diminished, though not altogether removed; and it is presumed there can be no difference of opinion about the propriety of reducing the danger so justly apprehended from colonization in India, to the least possible dimensions.

The admission of ships with cargoes from India into the Out-ports of this Country, would be injurious to the revenue, and in a still greater degree to the interests of our merchants and home manufacturers. The value of the annual imports from India according to the invoice prices, upon an average of six years from 1802-3 to 1807-8, (both inclusive,) belonging to the East India Company, to the commanders and officers of its ships, and to private British traders, amounted to £2,621,606.* Of the quantity of merchandise imported, at least three-fourths is always intended for re-exportation, and if it were not sufficiently obvious, what the actual state of the demand from foreign Europe must be under the enemy's vexatious and tyrannical decrees, its decline

---

* Printed Papers, page 56.

is manifest from the following facts:—First, That of 63,000 tons of shipping, which have been appropriated in the course of the last six years, by the East India Company to the private traders of the United Kingdom, only 16,230 tons have been employed:—and, Secondly, That, to say nothing of later arrivals, there were in the beginning of last July, in the Company's warehouses in London, goods of Indian produce and manufacture, worth £3,452,000, which had passed the public sales and for which no market could be found. These circumstances are mentioned for the purpose of shewing that the most unlimited freedom of trade would not afford any relief to the mercantile and manufacturing interests, which are now suffering, not from a deficiency of supply, but the want of sale; and that until the demand be restored, any addition to the stock of goods on hand would aggravate instead of alleviating the existing pressure. Such a change in the political state of Europe, as would open the markets of the Continent to the productions of India, can hardly be expected during the continuance of war, and when peace returns, the participation of other states in the commerce with India will materially interfere with the trade of this Country (however carried on), as the channel of foreign supply. The foreign demand for the goods imported by the Company, was chiefly to be ascribed at all times to their superior quality, proceeding from the advances given to the native manufacturers, and the care taken by the Company's servants abroad in selecting their home investments; whereas an open trade, by occasioning a sudden competition in the Indian markets, would produce a general deterioration of fabrics, and thus supersede the preference which British imports have hitherto enjoyed in the markets of continental Europe; while at the same time they would cease in their degraded state to operate as a stimulus to the rival skill and ingenuity of the British manufacturer.*

* The great superiority in quality which the goods imported by the Company bear over those imported by the private merchants, will appear from the following account (for which the author is indebted to the history of the commerce with India, by Mr. Macpherson, p. 422,) of the number of pieces, the amount of proceeds, and average prices of the Bengal piece goods, sold at the East India Company's sales in the under-mentioned years, on account of the Company, and on account of private merchants.

It has been already observed, that but a small proportion of the goods imported from India enters into home consumption. Some articles, such as silk stuffs,

Sold on account of the Company.			Years.	Sold on account of private Merchants.		
Pieces sold.	Amount.	Average Price.		Pieces sold.	Amount.	Average Price.
	£.	£. s. d.			£.	£. s. d.
350,329	648,756	1 17 0	1797	136,761	151,942	1 3 0
723,127	1,219,818	1 14 0	1798	127,810	182,594	1 8 6
334,115	508,584	1 10 6	1799 M.*	79,727	133,336	1 13 6
450,500	548,256	1 4 6	S.	152,870	145,503	0 19 0
1,129,501	1,406,879	1 5 0	1800	304,530	317,828	1 0 10
838,712	1,179,447	1 8 6	1801	396,444	379,569	0 19 1
437,862	660,019	1 10 0	1802	1,252,503	960,864	0 15 4
242,164	293,832	1 4 3	1803 M.	742,193	462,757	0 12 6
381,477	378,199	0 19 9	S.†	343,546	202,452	0 11 10
442,952	424,456	0 19 0	1804 M.	548,186	306,886	0 11 2
518,019	493,106	0 19 0	S.	431,013	220,082	0 10 2
174,321	142,157	0 16 6	1805 M.	320,727	193,665	0 12 0
None sold			S.	None sold		
410,196	336,453	0 16 5	1806 M.	113,233	67,453	0 11 10
199,500	146,456	0 14 9	S.	96,264	61,602	0 12 0

* M. denotes the March, and S. the September sale.

† At this sale 494,648 pieces belonging to the Company, and 501,293 belonging to private Merchants, were offered to the purchasers; but 113,171 of the former, and 157,747 of the latter class, were laid aside, there being no bidders. At some other sales still larger quantities have been withdrawn for the same reason.

The account has not been brought down to a later period, lest the subsequent depression of prices might be ascribed to the operation of Buonaparté's Continental system. The statement, as it stands, not only shews the preference that is always given to the Company's goods over those imported by private Merchants, but it also exhibits a gradually decreasing demand for the manufactures of India, arising chiefly from the improvements in the cotton manufactures of this and other countries of Europe, and a corresponding fall of price, owing in great measure, certainly to this cause; but in no small degree to the glut in the home market, occasioned by the excessive importation of the private Merchants, particularly in 1802, the year in which their privileges were extended.

and printed calicoes, are entirely prohibited, and the duties upon all are levied on so high a scale as to prevent their interference with the internal demand for our own manufactures. The duties, on muslins and nankeens, amount to £37 6s. 8d. per cent., and those on calicoes, dimities, and shawls, to £71 13s. 4d. per cent. on the sale prices. It cannot be disputed that these rates of duties offer a strong temptation to smuggling, and it is well known that even under the present system, notwithstanding all the checks which it interposes against fraud, an illicit traffic in articles of small bulk and great value, is carried on to a very considerable extent. In proportion as the checks are diminished, either in number or in force, the mischief will increase, until this branch of the revenue becomes insufficient to defray the charges of collection.

Government, however, would not be the only nor the principal sufferer from the growth of an illicit trade in articles of Indian manufacture. The British manufacturer would soon find a secret competition directed against himself, too powerful for all his industry and skill to withstand. The Bengal silks, the long cloths of Madras, and the chintzes of Surat, would secretly and insensibly find their way into our shops, our drawing-rooms, and our streets; and it would be but a slender consolation that the wearers themselves might possibly affect to lament the confusion and distress that had befallen the laborious artisans of Spitalfields, Manchester, and Paisley. Such an unexpected encroachment upon British industry, would provoke and justify a general clamour amongst those whose province was thus clandestinely invaded. Government aware, from the defalcation in its own receipts, that the complaints were not unfounded, would naturally apply itself to devise the means of relief. To lower the duties on Indian commodities would diminish the temptation to smuggling, but it would prostrate instead of upholding the already declining industry of the country; and in such a dilemma it is not improbable that, in place of protecting regulations, a total prohibition would be required, enforced by the terror of heavy penal inflictions. Here one cannot help remarking how singularly whimsical it is that British manufacturers, who are indebted to India for many of the raw materials on which their labour is employed, and who, even in their own markets, are so far from being able to maintain a fair competition with the Indian manufacturer, as to be obliged to seek shelter under protecting duties, varying from forty to seventy per cent. upon the value of workmanship, should after all set up a pretension of underselling their Hindoo rivals in the Asiatic markets!

The advantages of rendering the metropolis a general emporium, both for the export and import trade with the East, are great and manifold. The export cargoes, particularly to India, are composed of a variety of articles which must be collected from various parts of the country, and which are no where to be had in such choice and abundance as in London. The East India Company's sales, which take place at fixed periods, ensure a regular supply of the commodities both of India and China, not only to the British dealers, but to merchants, whom, in more favourable times, they invited hither from abroad, and who, during their stay in the metropolis, engaged in a number of other mercantile transactions, to the no small benefit of the general trade of the Country. When foreigners found it inconvenient to repair to London in person, for the purpose of making their purchases, the fairness of the Company's sales, and the known qualities of their merchandise, inspired them with such confidence, that they felt no uneasiness in intrusting their Correspondents with the execution of their Commissions, and the goods passed unpacked from one hand to another, on the Continent, merely upon the credit of the Company's descriptive marks. By the Act of 1793, teas cannot be put up at a higher price than the amount of cost and charges, and though a much higher price be always given by the buyers, the biddings are influenced solely by a regular demand, at no time increased by uncertainty of supply, a sufficient quantity being always on hand to prevent fluctuations in the market from the accidental loss of ships or other causes.

The private dealer knowing the extent of his custom, can calculate at every sale, within a few pounds weight the addition necessary to be made to his individual stock in order to meet the local demand for the current half year, on the expiration of which he is secure of receiving a fresh supply. In this way the practical evils incident to monopolies are guarded against, whilst the public reap all the benefits arising from the steady application of a large capital constantly employed in providing for their wants. The foreigner finding, that without capital and without risk, he can be supplied with the produce of the East through the channel of the English Company, on terms hardly less advantageous upon the whole than if he personally adventured in the Asiatic trade, is indisposed from envying either our political or commercial predominance. The British dealer is secured against the alternate recurrence of a scarcity at one time and a glut at another. The consumer is uniformly furnished at a fair price with articles unadulterated by fraud, and uninjured from long keeping; and in the collection of the *ad valorem* duties, the revenue has its full share of profit from the enhancement of price produced by competition at public sales.

No digested plan has as yet been proposed, in the event of the trade with India being opened to the British Out-ports, to protect the revenue and the fair trader against the effects of illicit commerce, and to secure to the Country either a continuance of those advantages which are at present derived from the publicity, fairness, and regularity of the Company's sales, or any equivalent, even in prospect, for the practical benefits which the Legislature is called upon to put to hazard. It is easy to propose restraints and not exceedingly difficult to frame fiscal regulations; but every person who is at all conversant with the collection of revenue knows that the ingenuity practised in evading Government duties, is at least equal to the skill of those whose business it is to enforce them. When a new tax is imposed, several years elapse before the mode of collecting it is so far perfected as to raise the produce up to the original estimate. It is now proposed, not to ameliorate, but to change the operation of a part of our revenue system (a system which, as applicable to the trade with Asia, experience has proved to be as perfect as any that can be devised) and the effect of the change, so far as it goes, will be to place the revenue under precisely the same disadvantages that attend any novel experiment in practical finance. The saving of carriage and commission that might be effected on the goods which are now purchased in London and conveyed to different parts of the Kingdom for home consumption, would be so exceedingly trifling as scarcely to be felt by the private consumer, and is quite beneath consideration in an extended view of the subject. Yet when we investigate the arguments of the Petitioners for an open trade with the Out-ports, if we set aside their merely theoretical reasonings on natural right, the odium of monopoly, and the general policy of leaving commerce completely unfettered by legislative interference; what besides this little practical convenience has been alleged in support of their claims? In looking at the other side of the question, considerations of far superior magnitude and weight press themselves upon our attention.

No proposition is more obvious, or likely to gain more general assent, than that every measure of policy is *prima facie* objectionable, in proportion as it tends to hurt the fair prospects of numerous classes of individuals, or to beget a great fluctuation and sudden decrease in the value of property: the risk of partial evil may no doubt be sometimes wisely incurred for the purpose of facilitating the attainment of general good; but still it is desirable that the value of what is hazarded should be fully known and duly appreciated.

The officers by whom the Company's ships are navigated, are men of high respectability and much nautical experience. Brought up in the service, their promotion is regulated by fixed rules; and the qualifications of each individual for the station he is entitled by seniority to fill, are strictly investigated before he is admitted to it. The Company's marine constitutes a sort of middle link between the Royal

Navy and the Merchant service. It has always happened at the termination of a war, that some officers of the navy who have been put upon half-pay have sought employment in the Company's ships, instead of entering the service of foreign states; and it is not unworthy of remark, that several persons who followed this course are now the ornaments of their profession and the boast of the Country. The Company's regular ships, 70 in number, employ 560 commanders and officers; their extra ships, amounting to 40, employ 140 more. To this list of 800 commanders and officers may be added 600 young men of respectable parentage and good education, who have entered the service as midshipmen, forming an aggregate of 1,400 persons, whose private prospects and professional utility in great measure depend upon the continuance of the trade in the present channel. The officers and clerks of every description employed at the India House, to the number of perhaps three or four hundred; the labourers in the Company's warehouses, to the amount of three thousand; and about twelve thousand tradesmen and artificers occupied in the supply of their shipping on the River Thames, would, together with their families, be reduced all of them to great difficulty, and many of them to absolute want. "Of what importance is it," says a wise and eloquent writer,* "under what names you injure

* Mr. Burke.

"men and deprive them of the just emoluments of "a profession in which they were not only permitted "but encouraged by the state to engage; and upon "the supposed certainty of which emoluments they "had formed the plan of their lives, contracted "debts, and led multitudes to entire dependance "upon them?"

Immediately connected with this part of the subject is the large capital (certainly much under-rated at 21 millions sterling*) vested in the Company's stock and warehouses, in the East India Shipping, the Docks, and other objects subsidiary to the trade, and in the trade itself, as now carried on, which would be depreciated in value to a greater extent probably than ten times the amount of all the profit on the new capital that an unrestricted commerce would attract. Should the trade be removed from the Port of London, the stock which it has created in and about the metropolis must be brought to the hammer, and the difference in such times as the present, between a direct signal of confiscation *(crudelem illam hastam)* and a measure involving compulsory sales is greater in name than in effect. *Sic par est agere cum civibus; non ut bis jam vidimus, hastam in foro ponere et bona civium voci subjicere præconis. At ille Græcus (id quod fuit sapientis et præstantis viri) omnibus consulendum esse putavit; eaque est summa*

* Printed Papers, page 154.

*ratio et sapientia boni civis commoda civium non divellere sed omnes eadem æquitate continere.**

Although it be admitted that the interests of individuals ought to give way to the great interests of the Commonwealth (care being always taken to provide an equitable compensation for whatever losses may be sustained in consequence of the accommodation), it is equally true, on the other hand, that in all political arrangements, national security is an object of loftier importance than mercantile gain. It is highly worth while, therefore, to examine what might be the effect of the extinction, or even of any considerable diminution of the Company's marine upon the essential resources and permanent stability of the British power, both in Europe and in Asia.

The advantages which may result to the State from the Company's naval establishment in future, (should the system remain undisturbed) will be best appreciated by a few cursory references to the services which it has rendered to the Country since the commencement of the war in 1793.

The ships employed in the Company's service are built and equipped with greater care, and at a much

---

* Cic. de Off. l. 2.

greater expense, than any other ships engaged in the commerce of the Country. They are adapted to the double purpose of trade and warfare, and though the rate of freight is necessarily proportioned to the expense of equipment, the additional charge has been much more than compensated by the security afforded to the property embarked in them.* Their own means of defence, also, have contributed not a little to relieve Government from the duty of otherwise providing for their protection. At the very beginning of the war, when the enemy's privateers were cruizing unmolested in the Indian seas, in defiance of the few King's ships then stationed in that quarter of the world, three of the Company's ships were fitted out as frigates for the purpose of keeping them in check, and giving more effectual protection to the China and country trade: a task which they performed to the entire satisfaction of His Majesty's

---

* An estimate may be formed of the saving under the head of insurance, in consequence of the superior equipment of the Company's ships, from the statement of the rates per £100. payable at Lloyd's on ships of different descriptions from Bengal to London, delivered on the 1st of June, 1809, to the Select Committee of the House of Commons on Indian affairs, by Mr. Grant Allen, and afterwards verified by Mr. William Bell, merchant and underwriter. From thence it appears that the ships taken up for the use of the private Merchants pay a premium of 15 guineas per cent. for the voyage from Bengal, while the Company's regular ships pay only 7 guineas, and their extra ships only 9 guineas, with a return of 2, for convoy.

Government, and of the King himself, who was pleased to bestow a special mark of his approbation upon Captain Mitchell, the Commodore of the squadron.

In 1795, when a large armament was fitting out for the West Indies, under Admiral Christian, in the difficulty of obtaining good transports, Government applied to the East India Company for the use of their ships. The request was readily complied with by the Company and the owners; and the commanders and officers cheerfully proceeded upon a hazardous and unfruitful service, by which they were thrown out of their regular and lucrative employment for the whole season.

The navy in 1796, requiring an immediate augmentation of force, and the ships then employed in the China trade being considered well adapted to supply the existing deficiency, the Company yielding to the convenience of the State, allowed the owners to dispose of a certain number to Government, who converted them into 64 and 50 gun ships.

In the same year, six of the outward-bound China ships, under the orders of Captain Farquharson, by dexterous manœuvring, deceived a French squadron, consisting of six heavy frigates, and by frightening the enemy from his station in the China seas, saved not only themselves, but a homeward-bound China fleet, which might otherwise have fallen into his hands.

In the years 1795-6 and 1796-7, that critical period, when all classes of people were vying with each other in loyal efforts to meet the exigences of the State, the Company raised 3,000 seamen for the supply of the navy, at an expense of £47,000.

Some of the Company's ships served in the expedition against Manilla in 1797; and in 1799, several more served under Admiral Rainier, in conjunction with His Majesty's squadron, when the Admiral bore ample testimony to the zeal, ability, and good conduct of their commanders and officers.

The Company in 1803 presented to Government the use of ten thousand tons of shipping, which was employed in protecting the coasts of the United Kingdom against the invasion then threatened by the enemy.

In 1804, a fleet of sixteen of the China ships, under Captain Dance, encountered a French squadron, consisting of an 84-gun ship and several frigates, which, after a severe engagement, were beaten off by the skill, judgment, and bravery of the officers and crews of the Company's ships, and property was thus saved from capture to an amount of not less than six millions sterling.

At the captures of the Cape of Good Hope, Ceylon, the Mauritius, and Java, the Company's marine was eminently conducive to the successful issue of the different expeditions, and its services have uniformly been acknowledged in terms of high approbation by those of His Majesty's Admirals, under whose auspices it has had the honour to act.

It would be tedious, and it is unnecessary to enumerate the many instances in which single ships have maintained gallant and successful struggles with privateers, and even with frigates belonging to the enemy, thereby occasioning a prodigious saving in the article of insurance. It is obvious, however, that had the Company's ships been of a smaller size, had they been less carefully equipped, or had the officers commanding them possessed less science and experience, they could neither have constituted an occasional resource to Government, nor exerted themselves with the same effect in their own defence.

At the breaking out of a war, the ten thousand seamen, composing the crews of the Company's ships, facilitate the manning of the navy. The liberal accommodation which large ships afford, conduces greatly to the health of the seamen; and in case of sickness, they have the additional recommendation of carrying medical officers, whose assistance cannot be afforded in vessels of smaller burden. It is only on board of ships of the highest class, that European troops can be sent to India, without being exposed to a severe mortality in the course of so long a voyage. The present channels of conveyance must therefore be kept up, if the lives of our men are to be preserved, or the security of our Indian possessions maintained. How far it is reasonable to expect that the East India Company shall maintain an expensive shipping establishment for national purposes, if they are to be deprived of all recompense as a commercial body, may be left to public justice and public candour to decide. The quantity of tonnage now employed by the Company, is much greater than what is required for carrying on their trade; and though it is impossible to state what proportion of it, in time past, ought to be assigned to their political account, or what saving they might in future effect under the head of freight and demurrage, were they discharged from the obligations arising out of their political character, it is indisputable that their commercial charges would experience a very considerable reduction, were the discontinuance of their exclusive privileges to be accompanied with a release from their exclusive burdens, and an exemption from the pecuniary sacrifices connected with them.* To withdraw the immunities

---

* On this subject the Select Committee of the House of Commons on Indian Affairs, observe, in their Fourth Report, (page 426)— "The shipping employed by the Company, have, in conformity "with their system, been for the most part, during a very long "period,

without removing the encumbrances, would be to commit an act of injustice without the temptation of benefiting from it, because a short-sighted policy in this, as in other instances, must inevitably defeat its own object.

In every view of the question, therefore, the Court of Directors have acted wisely in refusing to accede to the proposition for laying open the trade with India to the Out-ports of this Kingdom, and in so doing they have not consulted the interest of their constituents more than those of the empire at large.

Having thus endeavoured to point out (though

" period, constructed for warlike as well as commercial service; and " have been frequently, and in fact constantly used for political " purposes, either in the conveyance of troops and military stores, " or in expeditions against the possessions of the enemy. The part " of the freight, therefore, chargeable to the trade, can only be as- " certained by estimate. Further, a practice has prevailed, whether " correct or not your Committee do not pretend to determine, of " charging the largest proportion of the whole freight of the voyage " to the homeward-bound trade." The practice has unfortunately been as here stated, and has arisen from the Government and trade being considered as two branches of one concern, ministering to the wants of each other, and gradually becoming so blended, as to render a separation of the accounts matter of extreme difficulty. However, if the homeward trade is charged with three-fourths of the freight, and the Government with only one-fourth, (or nothing at all, as is now the case in most instances), for troops and stores sent out, it is evident, that upon a final separation of interest, a new and more equal distribution of charge must follow of course.

most imperfectly) the danger and impolicy of laying open the trade with India and China, it may be of use, while pursuing the same humble path of explanation and matter of fact, to notice the principal objections that are urged against the system under which that branch of commerce is conducted.

It would be superfluous even to glance at the old argument against the trade with Asia, founded upon its tendency to drain the states which engage in it of the precious metals, because the principle on which the argument rests, has long since been exploded as erroneous, and also because the principle, were it as just as it is universally acknowledged to be fallacious, would be inapplicable to the trade as it is now carried on by this Country.

The objections at present most in vogue are directed generally against the system of monopoly, and particularly against the alleged abuses of the monopoly held by the East India Company: and to these alone is it necessary to advert.

1st. In reference to the general objection against monopolies, it is well known, that from the year 1756, the privileges enjoyed by the Company in the Indian trade, have been continued, not so much for commercial objects, as to enable them to realize any surplus of territorial revenue that might accrue, and above all to maintain and preserve the connexion, which is found so advantageous to the paramount state, upon the only grounds on which it can safely rest. The exclusive trade to China has been conceded to them in like manner, with an enlightened regard to the geographical situation of that empire, its commercial intercourse with India, and the Company's services and sacrifices in maintaining the Indian connexion, as well as from considerations founded upon the peculiar character of the Chinese government and people.— It has likewise been shown, that the privileges enjoyed by the Company by no means form a *singular exception* to the otherwise uniform tenour of our national policy, but on the contrary, that the same spirit by which they were dictated pervades *many* of our laws and institutions. It may be farther urged, that at no time was the term monopoly strictly applicable to the privileges possessed by the Company, and that since the period of 1802, it has become an absolute misnomer. It is of the essence of a monopoly that the individual, or body possessing it, shall have the sole command of the articles in which it consists, with the power of withholding, or so disposing of them as to enhance their value in the market, and impose an arbitrary price upon the consumers. The Company instead of having a power of this sort, are obliged by law to bring to sale the commodities they import, *as early as possible*, and to dispose of them in moderate lots, at public auction, by inch of candle. No preference is given to their own goods, over those belonging to individuals, and the consignees or purchasers at the sales receive their goods immediately on payment of the duties and other regulated charges. Though the commerce is conducted on a large capital, the Company's stock is constantly in the market, and the sharers are as numerous or more so than they would be in an open trade. The books are at all times open for every description of persons of either sex, whether British subjects or foreigners, who may desire to become members of the Corporation, and who have money to adventure. In the General Courts of Proprietors, every one present has the same right with another to deliver his sentiments and give his advice. The only difference is in voting, and this difference is established on the basis of property, and graduated according to its amount. A Proprietor of £500 stock, has a right to attend and give his opinion. £1,000 stock entitles the holder to one vote by ballot—£3,000 stock to two votes—£6,000 to three votes—£10,000 to four votes, which is the largest number any individual is permitted to possess; and £2,000 stock qualifies any Proprietor for the office either of Director or Chairman of the Company. In no sense of the term can an institution so framed and regulated be called a monopoly; and after the extension allowed to the private trade in 1802, as already explained, this obnoxious appellation might be given with more propriety to several other corporate bodies, than to the East India Company.

II. It will not be contended that a mere transfer of any given portion of trade from one class of society to another, is productive of any increase of national wealth, nor will it be denied that the operation of withdrawing one set of capitals and substituting another set in the same branch of trade, is attended with loss both to individuals and the state. Admitting, therefore, the capital in this Country applicable to the trade with India to be greater than the actual trade absorbs, it by no means follows, even on purely commercial grounds, that the restrictions under which it is carried on, should be abolished, unless it can be proved, that they have been abused by that body in whose favour they *seem* to have been imposed. A qualified form of expression is employed, because the Company's privileges, have really been paid for at a price far exceeding their value.—Setting aside, however, this consideration for the moment, let us inquire whether the East India Company have, by their conduct, exposed themselves to the imputation of having abused their trust.—The most obvious mode in which this might have been done was by starving the markets in Europe and in India, for the purpose of enriching, by extravagant profits, the proprietors of India Stock. It is not denied by the claimants of an open trade, that there has been at all times a sufficient stock of Indian commodities in this country to supply the home market, and to meet the demand of foreign Europe. It is well known, that though the profits on imports from India have been extremely moderate, particularly of late years, the supply has usually been much greater than the demand; of which no other proof need be given than the fact already stated, of there having been at the beginning of last July, in the Company's warehouses goods of Indian produce and manufacture, to the value of nearly three millions and a half sterling, which had already passed the sales at the India House, and for which there was no vent either at home or abroad. Indeed the mercantile and manufacturing interests (as far as one can judge from their petitions and publications) seem disposed to rest their own pretensions and their arguments against the Company, chiefly upon the enlarged outlet which a free trade to the East would open to the produce of the soil and industry of this Country. It is of importance, therefore, to investigate the grounds, and the merits of this assumption. Now with respect to the grounds, they are not only purely hypothetical, but the hypothesis is directly at variance with the deductions of a long and uniform experience. Those articles which in this Country are accounted necessaries, the natives of India do not want, having cheaper and more desirable substitutes of their own; and as for our luxuries, their religion prohibits their use, or they are unable from poverty to purchase them. The East India Company have been indefatigable throughout the whole course of their commercial and political history, in their endeavours to introduce and diffuse European commodities among the natives of India, Persia, and Arabia; and with how little success their records will abundantly attest. Similar attempts were made by the French, Dutch, and other Europeans, with no better effect. The trade of the Americans with India, which has recently excited so much jealousy, has been confined to an exchange of bullion for goods. Even the private British merchants who are already engaged in the trade, and possess all the advantages of a personal knowledge, both of the most respectable tradesmen in this Country, and of the parties abroad through whose hands their shipments are likely to pass, together with large capitals enabling them to buy at the best markets, and to sell upon long credits, have already diminished, and in some instances entirely given up the exportation of goods to India. The average prices in the Calcutta market for a well selected assortment of goods, in which there must always be a large quantity of what are called perishable articles, such as beer, hams, cheese, &c., occupying a considerable space, have seldom yielded of late years a profit of more than 45 or 50 per cent. upon the whole investment when sent by the first ships, or of more than 30 or 35 per cent. when sent later in the season. The payments in India are generally made by equal instalments, at three, six, and nine months after the delivery of the goods in merchantable condition to the purchasers. The package and other charges in

England, amounting to a considerable sum, are calculated at prime cost, and the current rupee taken at 2s. 3d.; so that if the money be wanted to purchase a home investment, the bills must be discounted at a loss of from 10 to 12 per cent. per annum; and if the goods have been sold to a house in India of doubtful credit, a further premium is paid, for discount, of ½ or ¾ per cent. per month. The charges on sending out an investment to Bengal (which is reckoned the best market) may be thus stated:

Freight, insurance, duties, and landing, charges in India, short delivery, agency on the sales, remittances, &c.	35 per cent.
Loss on calculating the payments at 2s. 3d. the current rupee, and only prime cost on packages and charges	3
And if the proceeds are remitted in bills of exchange at 2s. 6d. the sicca rupee, 12 months after sight, or 18 months after date	7½
	£45½ per cent.

There are other incidental charges arising occasionally from the necessity of discounting the bills, &c., against all which there is nothing to place but the credit allowed in England, or discount for prompt payment on laying in the goods. On some commodities the freight and charges may be less than is above stated, but on goods that occupy little room the profit is proportionally smaller, and a very inconsiderable quantity of such articles is wanted to supply the market. Were unmixed cargoes of hardware, cotton goods, or of any of the great staples of this Country sent out to India, the returns would not equal one-half of the first cost and charges. If it be asked how the Commanders and Officers of the Company's ships contrive to render such a trade profitable, it may be observed, that they have many advantages over other traders: such as a saving of freight, commission, &c., and opportunities of trading from port to port in India. Of late years, however, they have gained rather by their passengers than their trade.

In answer to the objection that the Company are *unable* to compete with their rivals in providing the home investments, we may adduce the evidence given before the Committee of the House of Commons by a respectable merchant who lived thirty years in Bengal, and shipped goods on his own account to London. "The Company, from their "greater capital, and generally speaking, the better "intelligence and skill of their servants, are able "to carry on the trade with India with more ad- "vantage to themselves and to the country, than "individuals. I presume always, that the illicit

" practices of individuals are out of the question, and " that the trade is to be fairly carried on * * * *. " The Company's goods have a character for excel- " lence which the goods of private persons do not " attain. This gives the Company a considerable " advantage in the European market. A foreign " merchant can give his correspondent in London an " order to purchase the Company's goods, with con- " fidence that they will prove of the quality he " desires. With respect to the goods of individuals " he is at an uncertainty; he must trust to the judg- " ment and attention of his correspondent, and is " liable to disappointment in the quality of the goods. " The Company's goods, therefore, sell at a higher " price than the goods of private persons, even " though such goods may be equal in quality to the " Company's. When engaged on my own account " in correspondence to this country from Bengal, I " conceived the difference to be equal to fifteen per " cent. on piece goods, though my goods were pro- " vided with great care and attention. The com- " mission which falls upon the goods of private " merchants at the different places of purchase, ship- " ment, and sale, except where the owner himself " may reside, on the transit from the place of pro- " duce in Bengal through Calcutta and London to " the place of consumption abroad, by its repetition, " acts with a pressing weight upon the proceeds of " the goods, and abates the profit or eventually " creates a loss. Some of the rates of Commission

" were 10 per cent for procuring goods at the place " of manufacture, 2½ per cent for shipping, and " 2½ per cent on the gross sales in London."*

When due consideration is given to the difficulties with which the East India Company have had to contend in the prosecution of their trade, to the necessarily limited demand of the natives both of India and China, for the productions, whether raw or manufactured, of this Country—to the frequent absorption, in political enterprises, of those funds which would otherwise have been appropriated to commercial investments, the competition of private trade, the rival efforts of America, a state of long-protracted warfare, the prohibitory edicts of the enemy, and to the improvement in our domestic fabrics, which has in great measure superseded the use of Indian manufactures in this Country, it is matter of surprise that their imports and exports should have attained their present level, rather than that they have not reached a higher point. The select committee of the House of Commons, in their fourth report upon the affairs of the East India Company, have drawn a comparison of the actual extent of the Company's Trade, according to the produce of their sales at home, the prime cost of the goods

* Minutes of Evidence, 18th and 20th May, 1809.

imported, and the profit thereon, with the several estimates as presented to the House previously to the passing of the act of 1790, from which it appears that,

The annual extent of the import trade, according to the sale produce, was estimated in 1793, as follows,

India	. .	£2,314,900
China	. .	2,673,400
	Total	£4,988,300

The actual extent of the sale produce of goods from India, on the average of seventeen years, from 1793-4 to 1809-10 has been £2,637,746, exceeding the estimate by £322,846.

The actual sale produce of goods from China, on the average of the same seventeen years, has been £3,405,663, being more than estimated by £732,263.

The total gross produce of sales from India and China has been, on the average of those seventeen years, £6,043,409, surpassing the estimate by £1,055,109.

The extent of trade estimated in 1793, as to the prime cost of the goods imported, was

From India	. .	£1,121,300
China	. .	1,388,531
	Total	£2,509,831

The prime cost of goods imported from India has been, on the average of the above seventeen years, £1,356,490, being more than estimated by £235,190.

The average prime cost of goods imported from China, in the same seventeen years, was £1,597,474, being £208,943 above the estimate.

The total average excess of the prime cost beyond the estimate, has been £444,133.

The estimated profit in 1793, upon the scale of trade immediately in prospect, was

India	. .	£267,615
China	. .	636,919
	Total	£904,534

The average profits on the trade from India, during the whole period of seventeen years, was £309,561, exceeding the estimate by £345,013.

The average profits on the whole trade with India and China, has been £1,291,493, exceeding the estimate in the sum of £386,959.*

The actual prime cost of goods and stores exported by the Company to India and China, in the seventeen years commencing with 1793-4 and terminating with 1809-10, according to the same report of the Committee,† amounted to £28,237,048, giving an annual average export of £1,661,002.—Of this sum of £28,237,048, £5,883,320 was paid for stores, and £22,888,567 for goods.

The average export of seven years, 1791-2 to 1797-8, was to the value of £1,116,109.--The average on the ten following years, 1798-9 to 1807-8, was £1,877,290.—Upon this increase, however, the Committee observe,‡ that "the value of goods and "stores remaining on hand in India and China, "between 1804 and 1809, was to an amount very far "exceeding that on the antecedent years between "1792 and 1804, and what remained on the export

* 4th Report, pages 429, 430, 431.

† Ibid. page 437.

‡ Ibid. page 438.

" goods, on the 30th of April, 1809, amounted to " more than £900,000, *from which it is evident that " the Indian markets have been supplied to the utmost " extent of their demand, independently of consignments " made by private traders.* The increased residue of " stores does not appear so great in proportion as that " of goods, and is not liable to the same observa- " tion, &c."

The profit upon the sale of exports, calculated upon the prime cost and without reference to any charge on the consignment for freights, &c., amounted from 1792-3 to 1808-9.

To China . .	£266,404
India . .	837,940
	£1,104,344*

The promptness of payment on the part of the Company for manufactures, &c. exported by them, is noticed with just approbation by the Committee;† and the punctuality with which the payments have been made for the goods purchased at their sales, in which there appears to have been a deficiency of only

* 4th Report, page 436.
† Ibid. page 437.

£32,806, upon a demand of £103,386,489, is accompanied with the following remark: "It is satis-"factory to find in so extensive an amount, the defi-"ciency so small as stated, being only 7½*d.* per "Cent., which your Committee cannot but observe "suggests an impression highly favourable to the "management of this Branch of the Commercial "concerns of the Company."*

The Committee farther observe, that "the total re-"venue drawn by the state from those two branches "of Trade, during the seventeen years (from Ja-"nuary 1793, to January 1810), has amounted to "no less than £39,348,358, being on an average "£2,314,609, per annum, of which £399,555, was "on the Trade from India exclusively.—In the whole "Seventeen years the Duties on the Trade from "India, amounted to £6,792,434, being on the "average £399,555, as before stated. In the Eleven "years, ending January 1810, they amounted to "£5,054,170, or on the average £459,470, and on "the four years, ending January 1810, the average "was £525,005. The produce in the next year "was £457,489. It should be remarked that the "Export Trade of this Country in the several years "last mentioned, was involved in difficulties of an "unprecedented nature. Your Committee have been

* 4th Report, page 425.

" more particular in their explanations of the Duties " upon the India Trade, as that from China depends " much more upon home consumption; but the " average produce of Duties on the latter in the Eleven " years, ending January 1810, exceeded the average " of the seventeen years, in the sum of £525,721, " and the sum realized in the year, ending January " 1811, was more than that average by £1,788,012. " The produce of Duties and Customs on the whole " of the Trade from India and China in the year " ending January 1811, amounting to £4,160,555, " exceeded the average on the antecedent seventeen " years by £1,845,946: it likewise exceeded the " produce of the preceding year, by the sum of " £682,897. Your Committee entertain the greater " satisfaction in offering to the House, so favourable " a view of the productive powers of this very im-" portant branch of the Trade of the Empire in aid " of its resources, from being enabled at the same " time to State, that the Profit of the Company on " the whole of their Trade in the year ending March " 1810, was greater than in any year during the " whole period, with the exception of the years " 1800-1 and 1801-2."*

Whilst the source from which these Statements are drawn, leaves no room for doubt respecting their

---

* 4th Report, page 436.

authenticity, the facts they contain are the best refutation that can be given to the calumnies which have been so industriously circulated against the Commercial management of the East India Company. For though the estimates of 1793 were framed with a view to peace both in India and Europe, and the Country since that period has been engaged in continual war in both hemispheres, the Trade has far exceeded the expectations that were formed respecting it.

To those who are desirous of taking a retrospect of the Company's Commerce, for a longer period than that comprehended in the inquiries of the Committee, the following statement, the accuracy of which may be relied on, will not be unacceptable.

		Paid for Bullion exported. per Ann.	Goods & Stores exported.* per Ann.	Bills drawn on the Court of Directors. per Ann.	Sale of Goods. per Ann.
		£.	£.	£.	£.
From 1731 to 1741	aver. of 10 years	464,574	152,609	167,410	1,700,675
1741 to 1747	6	567,238	189,411	230,914	1,907,105
1747 to 1757	10	767,057	267,730	164,482	2,143,459
1757 to 1767	10	121,287	428,707	432,891	2,315,573
1767 to 1777	10	110,042	489,081	458,768	3,313,386
1777 to 1784	7	5,653	500,089	761,425	3,134,964
1784 to 1790	5	617,930	635,145	1,551,985	4,572,466
1790 to 1793	3	466,893	935,776	668,366	5,103,094
1794 to 1800 both inclusive	7	337,020	1,273,824	1,408,166	6,168,945
1801 to 1807	7	912,925	1,993,317	1,133,519	6,204,089
1808 to 1811	4	51,815	1,870,352	1,966,633	5,681,095

* This column of the account contains the invoice price of the Goods and

N. B. In the above account the amount received from Government for Saltpetre, is included down to 1784, and excluded afterwards.

The amount received under this head, from

1794 to 1800, average of 7 years per annum, was	£ 37,552
1801 to 1807, ditto ditto ditto	42,857
1808 to 1811, average of 4 years ditto	145,002

A particular analysis of the foregoing statement would require a minute survey of political events both in India and Europe, during the period which it embraces, and a detailed examination of their influence upon the trade. But a few observations which obviously suggest themselves upon a cursory inspection of its contents, will be sufficient for the purpose immediately in view.

In reference to the *Exports* it will be seen, that previously to the acquisition by the Company of territory in India, there was a large export of Bullion thither, and that the exports in Goods and Stores were comparatively inconsiderable, the imports both from India and China, having been at that time obtained in exchange for the precious metals.

In consequence of the Company's conquests during the war of 1756, and more remarkably still of the cession of the Dewannee in 1765, the nature of the intercourse with India underwent a great altera-

stores exported, which is 10 per Cent. added to the prime cost. In the statements of the Committee of the House of Commons, the prime cost is given.

tion, and the trade, instead of being conducted as before, on the principle of exchange, became a channel of remittance (either directly from India or circuitously through China to this Country) for the surplus revenue then existing after defraying the expenses of administration and internal government. The small quantity of Bullion exported was sent for the most part to China, and the remainder to Bencoolen, St. Helena, &c.

The exports in Goods and Stores about the same period, experienced an augmentation in some degree proportioned to the diminution in the export of Bullion, but the gradual augmentation down to this day is to be accounted for rather from the increased demand for European consumption, and the necessary supply of the governments abroad, than from the diffusion of British produce among the natives of those provinces that have devolved under our authority.

The renewed export of Bullion, from 1784 to 1790, was caused by the passing of the Commutation Act, the immediate consequence of which was an augmentation in the Company's imports of tea from China to the extent of ten millions of pounds weight annually, and for which Bullion was the principal medium of payment.

The export of Bullion from England, after declining between 1790 and 1800, was renewed to a great extent in the seven following years, owing to the wars in India, which not only absorbed the revenue of the territories, but occasioned a large accumulation of debt, which every exertion was made to reduce by this and other means.

In the four subsequent years, from 1808 to 1811, the exportation of Bullion by the Company almost entirely ceased, the commodities sent from England and India to China, having been more than sufficient to pay for their tea investments; and in the course of the last-mentioned period there has been a considerable reflux of the precious metals from Asia to Europe, which has come opportunely in aid of the treasury at home.

The Bills drawn on the Court of Directors have in part contributed to keep up the connexion between India and China, these bills having been frequently granted to individuals trading from India to China, who in return paid the proceeds of their merchandise into the Company's treasury at Canton, at fixed rates of exchange. In this way they have proved a convenient resource for the Company when the surplus revenue of their territories was absorbed by wars in India. But by far the greater proportion of those bills has been drawn in aid of the Governments abroad, and in liquidation of debts contracted by them in the prosecution of wars in India.

The large amount of Bills drawn between 1784 and 1790, and far exceeding the proportion of former periods, was occasioned chiefly by the expense incurred during the American war, in which the Company had to sustain an arduous contest with the native powers of India, assisted by the European enemies of Great Britain: a contest in which the success of the Company's exertions, tended in no small degree to support the honour and reputation of this Country, under the disasters which attended her arms in other quarters.

In the course of the seventeen years from 1793-4 to 1809-10, the Company's nett payments for Bills of exchange drawn from India and China, amounted to £23,493,054.* These Bills which have operated as a grievous burden upon the home treasury (as will be shewn more particularly afterwards) arose either out of the permission granted by the Court of Directors to their Governments abroad to draw upon them in liquidation of the Indian debt, or out of the option allowed to the Company's Indian creditors, of taking payment in England of the Interest half yearly, and of the principal when due of the loans advanced by them to the Company in India; an option of which they have availed themselves to a great extent.

---

* 4th Report of the Select Committee, page 438.

The Statement shews the *Sales of Goods* to have gradually increased, from 1741 to 1807, in the ratio of 17 to 42. From 1808 to 1811, the average scale rose to 56, notwithstanding the prohibitory edicts of the enemy, a fall of prices in the home market, and the great loss of Goods in the passage from India to Europe in the course of 1808-9.

It is to be observed, however, that but an imperfect idea of the Company's commercial enterprise can be derived from the statement; because in the first place, it does not comprehend the Sums which they have received subsequently to the year 1784, for Saltpetre delivered to Government, and, 2dly, because in this and various other instances they have sacrificed their own gains to the public accommodation.

The Sum received by the Company from the Board of Ordnance, for Saltpetre, between the years 1793-4 and 1809-10, amounted to £961,941; and during the same period the Company sustained a loss, by supplying Government with this article, to the amount of £436,689. Although by the Act of the 31st George III. cap. 42, they were only bound to deliver to the Board of Ordnance, Saltpetre to the extent of 500 tons annually, at the average prices at which it was put up at their Sales, (viz. the prime cost and charges) the actual deliveries have averaged 1,456 tons annually, and no allowance has been made them for this excess.*

The exertions and sacrifices made by the Company in encouraging the production of Indigo, Raw Silk, and Sunn Hemp, in their Indian territories, whilst they reflect credit upon their enterprise, have established in their favour an undoubted claim upon the gratitude of this Country.

In the early period of the Company's intercourse with Asia, *Indigo* constituted an important part of their home investments, but in order to avoid competition with the British Colonists in the West Indies, and the Southern States of North America, they afterwards discontinued the importation of that article. The cultivation of Indigo in the West Indies, having been relinquished about the middle of last century, in consequence of a heavy duty then imposed upon it, the trade fell into the hands of foreign nations, till the year 1779, when the Company directed their endeavours to renew its cultivation in their Indian territories, and in the course of a few years expended about £80,000, in the prosecution of that object. Having applied this powerful stimulus to its cultivation, the Company not only resigned the

* 4th Report, page 431.

trade to their own civil servants, and to the free merchants, who with their permission had settled in India, but supported them under the difficulties in which they were subsequently involved, by pecuniary advances to the extent of near a million sterling upon the security of their produce:* so that under the Company's fostering care, the value of the Indigo disposed of at the home Sales, has of late years considerably exceeded a million sterling annually, exclusive of large quantities that have been exported from India in the Country trade, and by American, Arabian, and other vessels.

Previously to the year 1776 the British manufacturers drew their supply of *raw silk* almost entirely from the southern countries of Europe. The soil and climate of Bengal being exceedingly well adapted to the cultivation of the Mulberry-tree, and to the rearing of the silk-worm, the Company have been unceasing in their exertions for the last thirty-six years, to render the British silk weavers independent of foreign nations for a supply of the raw material of their manufacture. Although for the ten years from 1776 to 1785, the Company sustained a loss of £884,744.† upon their silk sales, they steadily

---

* M'Pherson's History of the European Commerce with India, page 200.

† Ibid. page 223.

persevered under many difficulties in continuing and extending this important branch of commerce. The natives of India have been instructed in the Italian method of winding the silk, and the people occupied in the throw-mills of this Country have been employed by the Company in organzining it. Notwithstanding the vast increase in the cotton manufacture, which has greatly reduced the demand for silk, and the opposition of those concerned in importing organzined silk from the continent of Europe, there is now a regular importation from India of silk in its raw state, to the value of £600,000 annually:* and the supply may be carried to any extent, provided that the Company are duly protected against a preference to the produce of Italy and France.

If Great Britain still remains to a certain degree dependent upon foreign Europe for a supply of *hemp*, it is not owing to any remissness on the part of the East India Company to render available one of the most useful productions of their Indian territories as a substitute. In the year 1796 the Company commenced the importation of Sunn hemp, which grows in vast abundance in the Island of Salsette and in several districts of Bengal. They at first sold it without any view to gain, and even gave it away

* Appendix to 4th Report of the Committee of the House of Commons, No. 24.

to the rope-makers in this Country for the purpose of inducing them to make experiments of its strength and durability in different sorts of cordage. The result of those experiments was favourable upon the whole, for though it is rather inferior to Russia hemp, in the formation of small ship-tackling, it has been found better adapted to the manufacture of cables and large ropes, which occasion the principal consumption of hemp. In consequence of the differences between England and Russia which took place in 1800, the price of Russia hemp, which in 1792 had been sold at £23. 10*s*. having risen in 1803 to £61 per ton, His Majesty's Ministers urged the Court of Directors to promote the cultivation and importation of Sunn for the supply of the navy. Immediate instructions were accordingly dispatched by the Court to the Bengal Government to spare neither trouble nor expense in procuring an ample supply of an article from which great public benefit was likely to be derived; and hemp-dressers were at the same time sent out to India to teach the natives the best method of preparing it. But before the cargoes arrived an unexpected fluctuation in the politics of Europe had removed the obstruction to the acquisition of Russia hemp, and the Sunn was disposed of by the Company at a loss of £45,000. In 1807 the Directors proposed to Government to import for the use of the navy, and to deliver into His Majesty's storehouses, *without a profit*, as much Sunn as might be required, and the offer having been accepted, the importation has been continued upon this footing ever since. Another change in the political relations of Europe has again, in the course of the present year, opened the ports of Russia to the commerce of this Country, and a quantity of hemp is stated to have been already received from thence sufficient for two years' consumption. It is obvious that under such vicissitudes, added to the prejudices which oppose the introduction of every new article into general use, no discovery, however valuable in itself, can be productive of the same advantages which in different circumstances might be derived from it. The resource, however, is in existence;—the East India Company have shewn both alacrity and disinterestedness in exploring it and rendering it accessible;—and it now depends not upon them, but on the Government of this Country, whether its powers shall be stunted or developed to the utmost extent of their capacity.

Respecting the article of *cotton-wool*, which has sometimes been made a subject of charge against the Company, it is only necessary to observe, that as it is one of the staple productions of India, its cultivation requires no *special* encouragement. It is the raw material of one of the principal manufactures of that country, and has (particularly of late years) been exported thence in large quantities to China. The Company have also occasionally imported it into this Country, and have uniformly granted every facility to its importation on account of private merchants. It has been found, however, that from the length of the voyage and the high rate of freight payable in time of war, East India cotton cannot support a competition in the London market with that produced in the West Indies, Brazil, and North America. Yet Factories have been established by the Company, both in the upper part of India and in the province of Guzerat, for the purpose of ensuring a regular supply of this article in a clean state (for when it is brought home unpicked, it cannot possibly bear the charge of cleaning in this Country, superadded to the expense of freight), and should the war with America be unhappily prolonged, no disappointment is likely to occur for the future in obtaining a supply sufficient to answer all the demands of the British manufacturer.* But nothing can be more unreasonable than at once to compel the East India Company to admit the private merchants into a share of their trade, and at the

* To enable East India cotton to maintain a competition with that produced in Brazil or the United States, it is absolutely necessary that the duties should be levied *ad valorem*, instead of being levied as at present upon the weight. The former sells at from eight-pence to one shilling a pound, whereas the latter brings from eighteen-pence to two shillings, and the existing rate of duty is common to both; a circumstance which of itself establishes a preference in favour of a foreign article, to the discouragement of the produce of our own territories.

same time to dictate to the Company (as has been too often attempted) what goods they are to import and export. If the Company have in time past committed any fault in the conduct of their trade, it has been in too frequently deviating from the sound commercial maxim of dealing only in those goods on which a profit can be realized. In these deviations they have been actuated by a desire to benefit the State and to accommodate their fellow-subjects; but the boons which they have thus conferred, instead of being thankfully accepted, have in various instances been turned against them, either as weapons of attack or as means of extorting farther sacrifices.

Had the Proprietors of East India Stock received immoderate profits upon the capital they embarked in the trade, it might be urged, at least with plausibility, that the nation at large have a just claim to a participation in the gain; and that though, like other patentees, the Company might be entitled, at the out-set, to a fair reward for their skill and enterprise, the period for which the Patent was granted being nearly elapsed, it ought now, upon the common principle by which the dispensation of similar privileges is limited, to be suffered to expire. But the truth is, that in the present instance the Patentees have been uniformly the losers, and the Public the gainers; for the Patent was not, as in other cases, free and unqualified, but has been, in fact, (whatever may have been the intention of the donors,) clogged with conditions which have rendered it rather an onerous obligation than a beneficial license to the holders. This can hardly admit of doubt, when it is recollected that the India Stockholders have hitherto received little more than common interest for their money in a trade combining great political, with the most hazardous commercial risks. Mismanagement, indeed, on the part of the Court of Directors, is called in by the adversaries of the Company, according to their varying objects, for the purpose of solving this and many other problems. Supineness, carelessness, and extravagance, are represented as vices inseparable from all Joint-stock Associations, and, therefore, the East India Company, because it answers this description, by an awkward attempt at syllogistic reasoning, is pronounced slothful, negligent, and prodigal. "Every man thinks, Peter is a man, and therefore "Peter thinks:"—granted; but though an ass be an animal, and man may likewise be so denominated, it does not follow, by any law, either of nature or of logic, that Peter is the beast of burden so remarkable for sluggishness and long ears.

> Can Syllogism set things right?
> No; Majors soon with Minors fight,
> Or both in friendly consort joined
> The consequence limps far behind.

It is difficult to conceive why the Proprietors of East India stock should be more indifferent to their own interests, or less capable of discerning when their affairs are well or ill-managed, than any other body of men. The election of Directors takes place annually, and a meeting of Proprietors is held quarterly, to deliberate upon the general state of the affairs, and upon the conduct of their Representatives. The accounts of the Company's revenue and disbursements, and of their commercial receipts, charges, and payments, are regularly submitted to Parliament every year; and notwithstanding all these checks and the opportunities afforded by such publicity of proceedings for discovering misconduct on the part of the Directors, their management stands unimpeached, either by their immediate Constituents, or by the Legislature. Until the evidence of facts, therefore, is exploded, as unsatisfactory or obsolete, and inferences founded upon random assumption are sustained as a rule of judgment, the Company may surely be permitted to oppose their conduct (open as it is to investigation) to the unsubstantiated allegations of their adversaries. And if no instance of misconduct can be proved against the Company, all the arguments and claims that have been founded on supposed abuses, must necessarily fall to the ground; in as much as *de non apparentibus et de non existentibus eadem est ratio*, or in other words, as evidence not produced is the same as no evidence at all.

It being less the object of the Author of these remarks however to vindicate the East India Company against the imputations cast upon them by their adversaries, than to contribute to the general information, upon a question of great public importance, and to put the Legislature on its guard against a decision, which, though it may gratify the prejudices will be permanently injurious to the interests of the nation; it is material, with a view to this object, to consider the consequences which cannot fail to ensue, both to the Company and to the speculators who are likely to embark in the trade with India in the event of its being laid open.

The great objection to the argument employed by Lord Melville, in his Letter to the Chairman and Deputy, of the 21st March, 1812, (as quoted in page 31), is that the trade with India is *necessarily limited*, and that whether it be carried on by the Company, or by individuals, it never can be pushed beyond the demand which exists in India for European productions, and in Europe for the produce and manufactures of India. This demand is now amply supplied by the Company, and no individual exertions can greatly extend it. If a given capital be sufficient to carry on a certain branch of trade, it is obvious that any accession of capital is unnecessary, and therefore would be misapplied: and if the profits yielded by the same branch of trade, under judicious management, are barely adequate to pay the trouble and risk of the actual adventurers, it is equally indisputable that the only effect of additional competition will be to glut the markets, and ruin the competitors.

To those who have perused the Printed Evidence given towards the close of the last Session of Parliament, before a Committee of the whole House of Commons, on the Orders in Council, it must be apparent, that the speculations which were undertaken to different parts of South America, ignorantly and unwarrantably, no doubt, but naturally enough, at a period of great commercial stagnation, were the cause of distress and bankruptcy to numbers of our merchants and manufacturers. In the evidence of the Chairman of the Chamber of Foreign Commerce, at Birmingham, these speculations are represented to have been the effect not merely of rashness, but of absolute insanity; and well they might, if the passage extracted in a note below from an interesting work lately published by an intelligent observer, contains a correct account of the mode in which they were conducted.*

---

* "It may not be improper in this place to describe the conse-
" quences produced in Rio de Janeiro, by the excessive commer-
" cial speculations into which our merchants entered, immediately
" after the emigration of the Court of Portugal, and which could
" only be equalled by those which followed our expeditions to the
" Rio de la Plata.

" Owing

The author of the curious narrative, was an eye-witness of what he relates, nor does there seem to be any reason for doubting his veracity. The delusion

---

" Owing to the incredible competition, or struggle among our " merchants, who should send most ships and cargoes to a country " whose civilized population, exclusive of slaves, does not exceed eight " hundred thousand souls, (one-third at least of whom may be said to " make use only of what the land produces), it is natural to suppose, " that the market would be almost instantly overstocked. So great " and so unexpected was the influx of English manufactures into " Rio de Janeiro, within a few days after the arrival of the Prince, " that the rent of houses to put them into, became enormously dear. " The bay was covered with ships, and the custom-house soon " overflowed with goods, even salt, casks of ironmongery and nails, " salt fish, hogsheads of cheese, hats, together with an immense " quantity of crates and hogsheads of earthen and glass ware, cordage, " bottled and barrelled porter, paints, gums, resin, tar, &c. were ex-" posed not only to the sun and rain, but to general depre-" dation. The inhabitants of Rio de Janeiro, and more particu-" larly some of the Creolians and strangers from the interior, thought " that these goods were placed there for their benefit, and extolled the " goodness and generosity of the English who strewed the beach to a " great extent with articles for which their own countrymen had here-" tofore charged them such high prices. It is true, that the gentlemen " intrusted with these valuable consignments, did apply for sentinels " to be placed to guard the articles thus exposed, and their request " was immediately complied with. The result was such as might " easily have been anticipated from such watchmen, many of whom " did not fail to profit largely by the appointment. In the course of " several weeks the beach began to assume a less crowded appear-" ance; some few of the goods were taken to the residence of their " owners, others were removed; but to what place, or by whom, " there was no way of ascertaining; and a very great proportion

now existing throughout the Kingdom, founded on the advantages anticipated from a free trade with Asia, is, if possible, still more gross and prevalent

---

" was sold at the Custom-house *for the benefit of the Underwriters.*— " This stratagem so frequently practised (and certainly deserving " of the severest reprehension), afterwards operated as a very serious " injury to the regular sale of articles; for as the market was so " overstocked, scarcely any one would offer money for goods, ex- " cept at the Custom-house sales. As the depreciation continued, " numberless packages were there exposed for sale, in part damaged, " or apparently so. Indeed little more than the mark of a cord on " the outside of a single article, or a corner discoloured in a pack- " age, however large, was a sufficient pretext for presuming and " pronouncing the whole to be damaged. By means of this sen- " tence so easily obtained, great quantities of goods were brought to " the hammer in the Custom-house warehouses, under every disad- " vantage; thus the owners recovered the amount insured for, and " the insurers lost the difference between that sum and the price " they were sold at, also the attendant expenses. Many of the " Underwriters will, no doubt, retain a lasting remembrance of the " sales which took place at Rio de Janeiro, and other parts of South " America *for their benefit!*

" To the serious losses thus occasioned by an overstocked market, " and by the sacrifice of goods at whatever prices could be obtained, " may be added another, which originated in the ignorance of " many persons who sent out articles to a considerable amount, not " at all suited to the country: one speculator, of wonderful fore- " sight, sent large invoices of stays for ladies, who never heard of " such armour; another sent skates for the use of a people who are " totally uninformed that water can become ice; a third sent out a " considerable assortment of the most elegant coffin furniture, not " knowing that coffins are never used by the Brazilians, or in the " Plata. To these absurd speculations may be added numerous

than that which obtained some years ago, regarding the expected outlet for British commodities in La Plata and Rio de Janeiro; and if the new Par-

---

" others, particularly in articles of taste; elegant services of cut-" glass were little appreciated by men accustomed to drink out of a " horn or a cocoa-nut shell; and brilliant chandeliers were still less " valued in a country where only lamps that afforded a gloomy light " were used. Superfine woollen cloths were equally ill-suited to the " market; no one thought them sufficiently strong. An immense " quantity of high priced saddles, and thousands of whips were sent " out to a people as incapable of adopting them as they were of " knowing their convenience. They were astonished to see English-" men ride on such saddles, nor could they imagine any thing more " insecure. Of the bridles scarcely any use could be made, as the " bit was not calculated to keep the mule in subordination: these " articles were of course sacrificed. Great quantities of the nails " and ironmongery were useless, as they were not calculated for the " general purposes of the people. Large cargoes of Manchester " goods were sent out, and in a few months more arrived than had " been consumed in the course of twenty years preceding. No dis-" crimination was used in the assortment of these articles, with re-" spect either to quality or fineness, so that common prints were dis-" posed of at less than a shilling a yard, and frequently in barter. " Fish from Newfoundland met with a similar fate: also porter, " large quantities of which, in barrels, arrived among a people of " whom only a few had tasted that article as a luxury. How the " shippers in London, and other British ports, could imagine that " porter would at once become a general beverage, it is difficult to " conceive, especially when sent in barrels. These cargoes being " unsaleable, were of course warehoused, and of course spoiled.— " Newfoundland fish, that was generally sold at from twelve to " twenty dollars per quintal, was now unsaleable at four, and in " many instances did not pay warehouse-room. Earthenware was

liament have not wisdom, as well as firmness enough to resist the popular clamour, all the difficulties under which the country at present labours, will sink into

---

" perhaps rather more favourably received than many of the former " articles, for plates, &c. soon came into general use. Having enu- " merated various commodities which suffered a general deprecia- " tion, it may be sufficient to add, that many invoices of fancy " goods, and such as do not constitute a staple trade, were sold at " from sixty to seventy per cent. under costs and charges, and others " were totally lost. * * * * What must have been the delusions of " those traders who sent out tools, formed with a hatchet on one " side, and a hammer on the other, for the convenience of breaking " the rocks, and cutting the precious metals from them, as if they " imagined that a man had only to go into the mountains and cut " as much gold as would pay for the articles he wanted!

" Other evils resulted from these excessive and ill-judged specula- " tions to South America, which might naturally have been antici- " pated. The first was, that the produce was bought up with such " avidity, that many articles were soon double their ordinary value, " and continued to rise as our manufactures lowered. But this " was not all: the purchasers suffered equally from their ignorance " of the articles, as from their eagerness in purchasing them. For " instance, any kind of sebaceous matter was greedily bought for " tallow; and numberless hides spoiled in the drying, and eaten by " the grub, met with ready sale. Little attention was paid to the " state they were in; and thus it frequently happened, that lots and " cargoes of those articles, instead of reimbursing the adventurer, to " whom they were consigned, scarcely paid freight and charges. " This was also the case with coffee and other staple articles. Many " gentlemen more knowing than others, sent home lots of curious " wood, and even entered into the illicit trade of shipping the dye- " wood, which generally proved very disadvantageous, as the wood

utter insignificance, before the calamities that must result from blind and headlong compliance with the petitions which loaded the tables of its predecessor.

"of that species, grown in the vicinity of Rio de Janeiro, is very in-
"ferior in quality to that of Pernambuco from whence that trade is
"allowed by contract. The folly of speculation did not stop here;
"precious stones appeared to offer the most abundant source of
"riches; the general calculation was made upon the price at which
"they sold in London: but every trader bought them more or less,
"at the price at which they were offered: invoices of goods were
"bartered for some, which in London would sell for comparatively
"a trifle, as they were taken without discrimination as to quality or
"perfection: tourmalines were sold for emeralds; crystals for
"topazes; and both common stones and vitreous paste have been
"bought as diamonds, to a considerable amount. Both gold and
"diamonds were well known to be produced in Brazil; and their
"being by law contraband, was a sufficient temptation to eager spe-
"culators, who had never seen either before in their native state.—
"False diamonds were weighed with scrupulousness, and bought
"with avidity, to sell by the rules stated by Jefferies. Gold dust, as
"it is commonly called, appeared in no inconsiderable quantity,
"and after being weighed with equal exactness, was bought or bar-
"tered for. But previous to this, many samples underwent the
"following easy and ingenious process:—The brass pans purchased
"of the English, were filed and mixed with the gold, in the propor-
"tion of from five to ten per cent. according to the opinion which
"the seller had of the sagacity of the person with whom he had to
"deal: and thus by a simple contrivance, some of our country-
"men re-purchased at three or four guineas per ounce the very ar-
"ticle which they had before sold at 2s. 6d. per pound."

After adverting to the utter incapacity, from a variety of causes, of the mercantile agents, who were sent out to Brazil successfully

The hopes entertained at the period of the repeal of the Orders in Council, of a speedy adjustment of our differences with the United States, and of the revival of our accustomed trade with them, have been unfortunately frustrated by the

---

to conduct the affairs of their constituents, to the disputes which arose between them and the natives, and to the disappointments of the manufacturers in this country, from the failure of remittances, which brought many of them into the Gazette, and obliged others to change their consignees, with no other effect than a renewal of disappointment; Mr. Mawe observes:—

"Had it been possible to bring the whole trade to Brazil, under one "interest, many of those fatal consequences might have been pre- "vented. It should have been under the direction and control of "experienced merchants, who would have sent out such articles as "were known to be wanted, and whose agents would have been ac- "tively employed in obtaining intelligence respecting the population "of the country, its produce and consumption, particularly in goods "of English manufacture. Interest would naturally prompt them "to order and buy all that the country required, and return to this "country those articles which were most likely to answer the gene- "ral demand.

"If the trade had been properly conducted, we should have re- "ceived for a fifth of the produce which has been sold, the same "amount which has been paid for the whole, and it is certain, that "the purchasers would have been better satisfied; for to vend goods "at a reasonable price, is the certain way to keep the demand "steady, but to force them upon the consumer, whether he wants "them or not, is to render what was once a luxury, so common as "to become contemptible." *Travels into the Interior of Brazil, by John Mawe. London, 1812, pages 324 and 332.*

subsequent intervention of declared hostility. This event will probably increase the eagerness of the mercantile and manufacturing classes to seek indemnity for their disappointment in what they deem the rich and unexplored countries of the East. They will discover, however, when it is too late, that Nature has abundantly provided for all the real necessities of their inhabitants; that religion either prevents the growth, or prohibits the gratification of artificial wants, and that a singular structure of society, which neither the lapse of time, nor the revolutions attendant upon conquest, have been able to disturb, interposes insuperable obstacles to that species of expensive consumption and gainful intercourse which usually follow upon the diffusion of wealth in other parts of the world. They will find that the natives of India are not inferior in cunning, and all the arts of imposition to those of Brazil, and that the agents whom they may send out to superintend their sales and purchases, will have infinitely greater difficulties to encounter than they had in South America, from their ignorance of the languages and manners of the people. They will soon begin to feel the same effects from having their capitals locked up in India, or vested in unsaleable commodities in this Country, which have been felt by those who speculated to Buenos Ayres, and inundated Gottenburgh, Heligoland, and Malta, with West Indian produce, for which no demand was to be found. And after acquiring a little wisdom by dear-bought experience, they will perhaps acknowledge with Mr. Mawe, that it would have been better to leave the trade, as it is now carried on, to a Company of experienced merchants, who from an accurate acquaintance with the state of the markets, accommodate their transactions to the general consumption, than to turn it into a channel in which, through presumption, folly, and ignorance, it is likely to overwhelm the adventurers with a loss of four hundred per cent.

True it is, that this evil, like many others, has a tendency to correct itself in process of time. But is the intermediate ruin of a multitude of individuals, and the general waste of capital which it must occasion, matter of no concern or anxiety? Is a total derangement of a valuable branch of commerce so slight a mischief that it is not worth the pains of avoiding? Is every thing that has been gained by the skill and enterprise of the East India Company to be wantonly put to hazard in order to indulge a taste for extravagant speculation? And is the Company itself, when if not in the zenith of its prosperity at least in a train of extrication from its difficulties, after all that it has suffered and achieved, to be sacrificed to unmeaning clamour, the authors of which would be the first victims to the success of their own claims? It is incredible, even in this infatuated age, that a Legislature, not more famed for vigour than for prudence of counsel, can be smitten with such a degree of infatuation as to countenance, much more to sanction, a scheme so short-sighted and disastrous.

Reverting to the charges which are brought against the Company under the general head of abuses, it has been alleged both in and out of Parliament, 1st. that the Company have not fulfilled the agreement they made with the public in 1793, in virtue of which the public became entitled to a certain portion of the contingent profits derivable from their revenue and commerce, and on that account have forfeited all claim on the protection of the Legislature; 2dly. that their territorial revenues have been absorbed by a wasteful and losing trade; 3dly. that their frequent applications to Parliament of late years, whilst they furnish strong presumptive evidence of mismanagement have caused a serious addition to the burdens of the Country; and 4thly. that the Company is actually bankrupt, and ought to share the fate of other insolvent debtors.

The first objection, that the Company have failed in discharging the obligation imposed upon them by the act of 1793, of paying £500,000 annually to Government out of their profits, is founded upon an entire misconception or rather misrepresentation of the statute. Upon this subject, the Select Committee of the House of Commons in their Fourth Report have furnished satisfactory explanations, which shall be given in their own words.

"The sums stated to have been paid to Government in the years 1793-4 and 1794-5, amounting to £500,000, were two half-yearly payments, as prescribed by the act of 33d of the King, Cap. 52. Sect. 127. These payments standing alone, have led your Committee to inquire why the directions of the act have not been carried into effect in more instances."*

The following is the result of the Committee's inquiries.

"This stipulation was founded on an agreement between His Majesty's Government and the East India Company, that the public were eventually entitled to a certain portion of the profits accruing to the Company from the prosperity of their revenue and commerce. According to the mode of calculation laid down in the act, this conditional participation should accrue only from the following sources, viz. from the surplus remaining of the nett proceeds of the sales of goods at home, from the duties and allow-

---

* 4th Report, page 439.

" ances arising by private trade, and from all other " profits of the Company in Great Britain, after pro- " viding for the payment of bills of exchange already " accepted; for the current payment of other debts, " interest, and other outgoings, charges, and ex- " penses (the bond debt computed in another part " of the clause at £1,500,000 always excepted); for " a dividend on the capital stock at 10 per cent. per " annum, increased to 10½; and lastly, for bills of " exchange in liquidation of the debt contracted in " India, to the extent of £500,000 per annum. " Provision having been made for these several pay- " ments, the annual sum payable to the public in the " way of participation, was fixed at £500,000, to " be set apart half-yearly, on the 1st July and the " 1st January in each year, beginning with July, " 1793. Provisions were likewise made in the act " to ensure punctuality in the payment of these sums " into His Majesty's Exchequer; but it was enacted, " that in the event of a deficiency in the amount of " the proceeds (after making the payments to which " precedence was given) arising from extraordinary " expenses incurred in time of war or preparations " for war, or from circumstances incidental to war, " that the deficiency or deficiencies were not to be " made good from the surplus of the future year or " years, but were to be deemed a debt to be made " good to the public at the determination of the ex- " clusive trade of the Company, in case their general " assets should be more than sufficient for the pay-

"ment of all their just debts, and for making good "the value of the capital stock, rated at £200 for "every £100 of such stock.

"The payments shewn in the years 1793-4 and "1794-5, from having been made when a deficiency "of funds for the purpose, according to the prin- "ciple of participation laid down, is fully apparent, "your Committee think it right to state to the "House, that a reference to the 124th section will "furnish an explanation of the transaction, by "shewing that the payment was specifically directed "to take place antecedent to the addition of the ½ "per cent to the dividends of the capital stock, and "that it must be considered to have been made from "the balance of cash in the hands of the Com- "pany, distinct from their nett proceeds of the "year.

"As to the sources from which the participation "of the public was to be derived, namely the surplus "proceeds, &c. as described in the beginning of the "section, your Committee cannot avoid reverting "to the estimates on which this arrangement was "evidently founded, and again remarking, that the "supply of a million annually from the surplus re- "venue in India, as directed in the 107th section, "must have been assumed as the basis of the expecta- "tions then held out to the public, because it seems "clear that the surplus proceeds in contemplation by

" the 111th section of the enactment, were in reality " the combined profit derived from revenue and " commerce. And this conclusion is farther sup- " ported by provision being made for failure of pay- " ment in the event of a deficiency of surplus pro- " ceeds, happening from war. As the deficiency " which has, in fact, existed from the time of passing " the act, is to be ascribed to the wars in India and " Europe, no farther payment has been made to the " public under the directions of the act, but your " Committee observing that in some years a surplus " of funds is shewn in the account, notwithstanding " the war (after making the payments for dividends, " and on bills of exchange for Indian debt) have " thought it necessary to ascertain and to state to " the House, the causes why payment was not made " on the participation of such years.

" The payments stipulated by the act, consider- " ably exceeded the funds in the first year from " which such payments were to be made, conse- " quently recourse was had to funds that could on no " consideration be looked upon as profit, the only " source from which the proceeds described could be " derived. The excess of payment thus made, was " supplied by moneys raised by the Company, either " on new capital or on bond, in excess of the " £1,500,000, to which that debt was then limited, " and became a debt payable from the nett proceeds, " taking priority of the public claim to participation.

" The deficiency of funds for the liquidation of this " claim is shewn by an account inserted in the ap- " pendix.

" From a variety of circumstances, therefore, but " chiefly from those consequent upon war, the nett " proceeds of the Company's treasury in Great Bri- " tain, have not been sufficient for the payment of " the participation to the public according to the " act, and with the exception of the sum of " £500,000, paid in the manner above described, the " whole has fallen in arrear, and become a debt due " by the Company under the 122d section, subject, " however, to the reservation contained in the act as " to the liquidation of it, that is *in the event only of* " *the Company's general assets amounting in value to* " *more than sufficient for the payment of all their just* " *debts, and the realization of their capital stock.*"*

The second objection, that the territorial revenues of the Company have been absorbed by a wasteful and losing trade, is a favourite one with two descriptions of persons—the advocates of the political system which was acted upon in India during the administration of Marquis Wellesley, and the petitioners for a free trade. The former contend that all the expense incurred in wars, or consequent upon other

---

* 4th Report, page 448.

measures terminating in the aggrandizement of the British empire in India, has been much more than compensated by the revenue derivable from the conquered and ceded territories. The latter maintain that they can carry on the trade to much greater advantage than the Company; and, espousing the foregoing doctrine as convenient for their purposes, they likewise assert, that by exonerating the Company from a commerce unprofitable and ruinous as it is now conducted, and by leaving their attention exclusively directed to the administration of their territorial revenues, the surest foundation would be laid for the future prosperity of the Company.

It is altogether foreign to the intention of the writer to enter into political controversy. Lord Wellesley's system may deserve every panegyric which his warmest eulogists have ever passed upon it; and in some respects too much cannot be said in its praise. But those who argue as if the tendency and operation of his system had been defeated by the commercial mismanagement of the Company, however they may affect to extol, are, in truth, the greatest disparagers of that distinguished statesman.

The objection, with whatever view it has been brought forward, is effectually repelled by the reports of the select Committee of the House of Commons and by other authentic documents. The Committee have stated in their 2d Report, that on a comparison with the estimates in 1793, the result of the actual accounts of the revenues and charges of India in 1808-9, was more unfavourable than the estimate, in the sum of £1,189,619, the estimate having calculated on a surplus revenue of £1,163,577, and the actual accounts of 1808-9, having exhibited a deficiency of £26,042. The difference is stated in a general way to have arisen as follows.

	Estimate 1793.	Actual Accounts, 1808-9.	Increase.
	£.	£.	£.
Revenues	6,962,635	15,525,055	8,561,430
Charges of Government .	5,188,125	13,151,224	7,963,099
Nett Revenue	1,775,500	2,373,831	598,331
Supplies to Bencoolen and Penang, &c. . . .	50,000	158,208	108,208
Interest on the Debts. .	561,923	2,241,665	1,679,742
Total	611,923	2,399,873	1,788,950
Surplus Revenue . . .	1,163,577		
Surplus Charge . . .		26,042	
Deterioration as shewn above			£1,189,619

" From this view it is ascertained that, although " the revenues have increased in the sum of " £8,561,430, the increase in the charges of

" Government has been such as to absorb the whole " except £598,331, and that the additional supplies " to Bencoolen, &c., but, by far in the highest de- " gree, the increase of the interest on the debts, have " contributed to prevent the exhibition of a surplus " revenue, as by the estimate of the year 1793."*

The disproportionate increase of charges, is imputed by the Committee, to additional naval and military establishments, required in consequence of the new acquisitions of territory, and likewise to stipends and payments to the native princes of India in fulfilment of treaties concluded between them and the Company.

To an exposition of the state of the Company's finances at home and abroad, submitted to the select Committee of the House of Commons, on the 1st of April, 1808, by the Court of Directors, an account was annexed, shewing the amount of the Indian revenues and charges, and of the surplus or deficit of the former, from 1793-4 to 1807-8 inclusive, together with the state of the Indian debt through the same space of time. From this account the following extract is made in the document referred to, for the purpose of illustrating the position, that though the revenues of India have greatly increased, the expenditure has risen in a still greater degree. For

* 2d Report, page 62.

in 1793, when the revenue was only eight millions per annum, there was a surplus of £1,600,000; while in 1807-8, the second year of peace, when the income had advanced to fifteen millions a year, there was a deficiency of £1,019,097.

	Revenues.	Charges.	Interest.	Surplus.	Deficit.	Amount of Debt.
	£.	£.	£.	£.	£.	£.
1703-4, First Year of the Company's new Charter	8,276,770	6,066,923	526,205	1,683,642	- -	April, 1793, 7,971,668
1798-9 - - - -	8,652,032	8,417,812	759,326	- -	525,106	Do. 1798, 10,866,588 Do. 1799, 12,811,863
1802-3 - - - -	13,464,537	11,043,108	1,577,922	843,507	- -	Do. 1803, 19,523,737
1805-6 - - - -	15,217,516	15,561,330	2,070,792	- -	2,414,606	Do. 1806, 28,538,804
1807-8, per estimate	14,614,261	13,436,198	2,197,160	- -	1,019,097	Do. 1808, 31,895,000

" The commercial charges and supplies to Bencoolen, &c. are " not here included. The charges are the amount *paid* in the re- " spective years, as stated in the Budget Accounts.

" What is most obvious and striking in this state- " ment, is the increase, not of the charges only, but " also of the debt, as the revenues increased, and " not merely in proportion to the increase of the " revenues, for, whilst from the year 1793-4, to the " year 1805-6, the amount of the revenues has not " been quite doubled, that of the charges has been in- " creased as five to two, and that of the debt nearly " quadrupled, besides a very large sum of debt trans- " ferred in the course of that period to England. " The greatest increase under all these heads, has " been since the years 1798-9. The first foundation

" of the debt was laid by the Mahratta war of 1778. " The accumulation of that debt and of charges, may " in most part be accounted for by the foreign expe- " ditions undertaken from India at the desire of His " Majesty's Ministers, the two wars of Mysore, the " two wars of 1803-4 and 5 with the Mahratta chiefs, " and the permanent increase of military establish- " ments occasioned by these events, and other political " measures of the same period."*

The select Committee of the House of Commons, for the express purpose of ascertaining whether any part of the unfavourable balance now existing against the Company upon the whole concern, is attributable to losses upon their trade with India, have endeavoured, as far as was practicable, in their third report, to separate the political from the commercial part of the Company's affairs, by drawing out an adjusted account, exhibiting on one side the supplies by India to England, and on the other, the supplies from England to India, between the year 1792-3 and the year 1808-9, and thus striking the balance between the two. The following abstract of this account is given at the conclusion of the third report.†

---

* Exposition of the State of the Company's Finances at Home and Abroad, ordered by the House of Commons to be printed, 22d May, 1810, page 6.

† Page 373.

Supply by India to England.

	£.	£.
Investments of goods	25,407,099	
Sundry advances for Bills, &c. repayable in England	2,329,236	
	27,736,335	
Commercial Charges not added to the Invoices	2,916,279	
Nett Amount of Supply to Canton .	3,313,654	
		33,966,268
Advances and Charges in India, admitted as Claims upon the Public, and paid in England by His Majesty's Government		8,212,372
Total supply by India to England		42,178,640

Supply from England to India.

	£.	£.	
In Goods and Stores—the total amount of the Consignments as credited in the Indian Books .		11,554,218	
In Bullion, as Do.		7,360,752	
By Bills of Exchange		14,746,038	
Sundry Receipts for which England is credited.		393,372	
Total credited to England in the Indian Books		34,054,380	
Add			
Disbursements of His Majesty's Paymasters General on account of regiments serving in India, 1793 to 1807 . . .	2,638,988		
Victualling Office Demands	80,024		
Interest allowed on repayments by Government	841,900		
	3,560,912		
Charges paid in England, supposed to be territorial	6,193,049		
		9,753,961	
Total return by England to India			43,808,341
From which, deducting the supply by India, stated above, the balance will appear in favour of England, in the sum of			£1,629,701

which is the amount in which, upon the principles now acted upon, the Political may be stated to be Debtor to the Commercial Concern during the period in question.

The select Committee, in their Fourth Report,* have stated, that the Company's nett profit upon the whole of their trade, between 1792-3, and 1808-9, abroad, and between 1793-4, and 1809-10, at home, has exceeded by £2,164,533 the amount required to defray the expenses and losses immediately incident to it, and to pay the dividends on the capital stock with the interest on the bonds, although the total prime cost of the goods lost by the Company from shipwreck, in 1808, and 1809, amounted to £886,168, and the total cost and computed profit of these goods to £1,202,638.† It is clear, therefore, from these statements—1st, That so far from the revenues of India having been absorbed by the commerce of the Company, they have actually drawn from it the sum of £1,629,701,——and 2dly, That a surplus profit upon the whole trade of the Company, to the amount of £2,164,533, has been applied to the relief of their general finances.

The 3d objection, that the frequent applications made by the Company of late years to Parliament for pecuniary aid, have caused a serious addition to the burdens of the country, requires attention to the political events which have occasioned the Com-

* Page 454.

† Supplement to the Exposition of the state of the Company's Finances, ordered by the House of Commons to be printed, 22d May 1810.

pany's embarrassments, as well as to the circumstances under which their several applications for relief have been preferred.

The whole of the Company's financial difficulties are to be ascribed to the almost unceasing course of hostilities, which for twenty years has raged in Europe, and to the frequent wars which the Company has, during the same period, carried on in India.

The increased expense incurred by the Company in time of war, under the head of freight and demurrage alone, amounts to about £600,000, annually; and during the whole period of their charter, it may be estimated at twelve millions sterling.

The rise in the rate of wages in England, consequent on taxation, and other causes, has greatly enhanced the price in the home market, of every article which the Company exports; and as the sale prices abroad have not advanced in any proportionate degree, a corresponding reduction on the profits of their exports has arisen, which has not by any means been compensated by the prices they have received for their imports.

Besides these inconveniences which they have felt in common with the nation at large (inconveniences however under the pressure of which other merchants have repeatedly sought and obtained parliamentary relief), the Company have had to struggle with difficulties and hardships peculiar to them as a body.

The effects of long protracted warfare are manifest in the prodigiously enlarged scale of their military expenditure. In 1793, the military charges of India, including buildings and fortifications, were estimated at £3,035,375. The actual military charges in 1798-9, including buildings and fortifications, amounted to £7,659,791, shewing an increase, beyond the estimate, of £4,624,416*. The number of King's troops which the Company were bound by act of Parliament to pay and maintain for the defence of their Indian possessions, was 10,727, the annual expense of which would have been about £485,000. Since the year 1798, the extent of that force which forms the most expensive part of their military establishment, has been gradually increased; and in 1810, the number of King's troops in India amounted to 21,763. The increase of expense consequent on this augmentation of force, in the twelve years, from 1799, to 1810, has been £3,958,850, exclusive of the expense of horses for His Majesty's cavalry, stores supplied to all the regiments, and other contingencies, which if included would

---

* Second Report of the Select Committee, page 38.

raise the total excess of charge in India, probably to £4,500,000. And if Indian interest were charged on the annual excess of expense, it would make a total of £6,200,000.

At home, the charges of the Pay-office against the Company are necessarily swelled by the excess in the numbers of His Majesty's troops in India, allowed by the acts of 1788 and 1791. Those acts provided for one regiment of dragoons, and nine regiments of infantry, the expense of which, as charged in the Pay-office accounts, was about £75,000 per annum; or for 18 years, £1,350,000. The difference between this and the sum actually charged, exceeds two millions sterling, without interest.

The Company have been also charged with the expense of a recruiting company at home, though the recruits so raised are often sent not to India, but to other quarters; and in several instances the pay of Colonels of regiments employed at home, or on the continent, have been charged to the East India Company.*

It has always happened, that when Great Britain has been involved in European war, its effects have been felt in India. Even when no Euro-

* Printed Papers, page 127.

pean enemy appeared in the field, either to threaten the security of the Company's territory, or to dispute the predominance of their power, their resources have uniformly been applied under the authority and direction of His Majesty's Government, to frustrate schemes from which danger was apprehended to the general interests of the empire, and to undertake conquests, which though important in a national view, were certainly not worth to the Company the expense incurred in their acquisition. Wars growing out of our Indian system, particularly since the period when ambition seems to have obtained an ascendency over prudence in our councils, the territorial revenues of India are perhaps inadequate to provide for; but it would be altogether extravagant to expect that they can be equal to support European wars, for general and national objects, or a struggle between Great Britain and France, on the soil of India, for the maintenance of power in Europe.* It is well known, however, that in the course both of the last and the present war, the Company have not only had to contend against France and her allies on the Continent of India, but that expeditions have been

* Letter from the Chairman and Deputy, to the Right Hon. Robert Dundas, dated 16th September, 1808. Printed Papers, page 9.

fitted out by the Company against the French, the Dutch, and the Spanish possessions in the Indian Archipelago, and that a large force was sent from India to the Red Sea, which assisted in the expulsion of the French from Egypt. And it is equally true, though not perhaps so well known, that the Company have been only partially indemnified for the cost of enterprises, undertaken by the express command of His Majesty's Government, and for objects as decidedly national, as if they had been directed against Martinique, Curaçoa, Trinidad, or the Coast of the Mediterranean. Though the Moluccas were restored to the Dutch at the Peace of Amiens, the Company were allowed only half the expense of their capture. The same rate of indemnification was adopted in regard to Ceylon, notwithstanding that it has been made a King's settlement. And from the expense incurred by the Company, in the Egyptian expedition, the nett ordinary pay of the troops employed was deducted in the indemnity awarded them, though the place of the native troops was immediately supplied by new levies in India. Nay, two of His Majesty's regiments of infantry, which had formed part of the expedition, returned from Egypt to Europe at the termination of the campaign, clearly shewing that they had not been sent out for the defence of India.

The still unliquidated claim of the Company upon the public for these services is,

For Ceylon, 1796-7 to 1801 -	£1,205,656
Eastern Islands, 1795-6 to 1805-6	1,321,859
Egyptian Expedition, 1798-9 to 1802-3	120,000
Total	£2,647,515

with the interest since accumulated upon that sum.*

The extra expense recently incurred in the capture and on account of supplies to the Mauritius and Java, amounts to,

Mauritius - - -	£2,127,672
Java - - - -	1,502,411
Together - -	£3,630,083

The natural, and indeed the necessary consequence of war expenditure has been the same in India as in Europe. According to the adjusted statements in the Reports of the Select Committee of the House of Commons, the Company's debt, which in 1792 did not amount to eight millions, had grown in 1808 to near twenty-nine millions sterling, in spite of every effort on the part of the Court of Directors, not only to check its increase, but also to accomplish its reduction.—Of these endeavours, the Select Committee have

* Third Report, Appendix, No. 17, page 396.

expressed themselves in terms of just commendation in their Third Report.*

"The anxiety with which the increase of the "debt in India has been contemplated by the autho-"rities at home, is strongly evinced by a Letter ad-"dressed to the Chairman, and Deputy Chairman of "the Court of Directors, by a late President of the "Board of Commissioners, for the affairs of India, "when quitting that department in 1801, which is "already upon the Table of the House. The sug-"gestions contained in it were not neglected by his "successor; and in the next year, exertions were "made to carry into effect a part of what was re-"commended in that document. The general prin-"ciple of the measures (which were apparently con-"fined to the space of two years), was to accomplish a "more rapid liquidation of the principal of the Indian "debt, than could be effected by the existing ar-"rangements. The proposed plan being brought to "maturity, a communication of it was made to the "Bengal Government, by a letter, dated 1st June, "1803, with orders for carrying it into execution. "This document will likewise be found in the Ap-"pendix; and the amount of the exports of goods "and of bullion in the years 1803-4 and 5, will prove "that every effort was made to ensure the success of

---

* Page 371.

"the measure. The accumulation of the Indian "debt, however, which appears in subsequent years, "shews its entire failure. The cause of this your "Committee attribute to the war with the Mahratta "Chieftains, which broke out in the very year in "which the plan commenced, and did not finally "close till April, 1805."

From the 1st March, 1803, to the 1st March, 1806, the Company's supplies to India and China exceeded the amount sent in the three years immediately preceding, in the sum of £2,712,526, and the amount of their receipts for the sale of goods, from the 1st March, 1803, to the 1st March, 1806, fell short of the receipts in the three years immediately preceding, in the sum of £3,268,671.* These facts, which are to be accounted for from the absorption not only of the revenues of India, but of the home supplies by the Mahratta war, sufficiently evince the anxiety felt by the Company for the liquidation of their Indian debt, and at the same time shew, that besides the disappointment of a favourite hope, they experienced an unprecedented failure in an usual source of income from a political measure, in which they were no ways implicated, and of which they always disapproved.

---

* Exposition of the East India Company's Finances, ordered by the House of Commons to be printed, 2d March, 1810, pages 3 and 4.

The extinction of the surplus revenue of India from which a million sterling annually ought to have been appropriated to the purpose of commercial investment, was not the only baneful effect produced by the increase of the debt. The terms on which the loans in India were contracted for of late years, have tended to transfer the burden of the debt from the territories abroad to the Company's funds at home.

Of old, the principal and interest of the sums borrowed were payable only in India, and consequently the pressure of the debt fell chiefly upon the Indian treasuries. But in the course of the ten years, from 1798 to 1808, the loans were made with an option to the lenders, of demanding bills upon England, for the interest, half yearly, of their subscriptions, and also for repayment of the principal at the periods when the loans became redeemable, which were usually at the expiration of ten years, from the dates of the contracts. A general reduction in the rate of Indian interest, from 10 and 8 to 6 per cent., operated as an inducement to the Company's creditors to avail themselves of the option of receiving payment in England, and bills for a sum exceeding thirteen millions sterling, have been drawn by the Governments in India upon the Company's treasury in London, between the 1st May, 1807, and the 3d February, 1812, on account of the interest and capital of the Indian debt, exclusive of the sums that have been re-invested at home in the Company's securities. This transfer of debt, though it must from the reduction in the rate of interest, have produced an important improvement in the general concerns of the Company, has also caused a severe pressure upon their finances in England, and is in fact the source of all their late embarrassments. When the Government of this Country borrows money to supply the public exigencies, the interest only is to be provided for, as they are never called upon for repayment of the capital. But the Company by the conditions of their Indian loans, have been obliged to provide for the discharge both of capital and interest, and that too in England, where there are no funds properly applicable to the liquidation of their territorial debt. Hence the necessity of their applications to Parliament of late years for relief.

Let us trace the amount of pecuniary assistance which they have at different times obtained, and the grounds on which it has been voted.

In 1805, when the Company's difficulties first began to press upon them, they applied to Parliament for payment of a large balance, amounting to £5,570,336, due to them from Government on account of advances for the public service in India. The account having been referred to a select Committee of the House of Commons, they reported, that after dividing the charges of the capture &c. of Ceylon, and the Eastern Islands, equally between the public and the Company, deducting the ordinary expenses of the troops employed in Egypt, from the gross charges of the expedition, and taking credit for the whole amount of charge against the Company, by His Majesty's military Pay Office, many articles of which the Committee allowed to be objectionable, there was a clear balance owing to the Company of £2,300,000. Of this sum one million was paid to the Company on account in 1805, and another million in the following year.

By the Act of 37th of the King, cap. 3, the Company were permitted to add two millions to their capital stock, a power of which they have never chosen to avail themselves; because this addition to their capital could hardly have failed to depress the value of their stock in the market, and because the dividends which they must have paid to the new proprietors would have borne a much greater proportion to the sum raised by subscription, than the legal rate of interest bore to the same sum, if borrowed on loan, or raised in another way. Accordingly an act was passed in 1807,* to enable them to borrow two millions upon bonds, by which means they got over their difficulties in that year.

In 1808, the Company submitted to Parliament

* 47th George III. cap. 41.

an exposition of their finances at home and abroad, and solicited payment of a sum of £2,460,000, due to them from the public. This document was referred to a select Committee of the House of Commons, who reported, that they found £1,500,019, unquestionably owing to the Company, a doubtful balance being still left open for discussion. The Committee at the same time stated, that they would have been disposed to recommend a more liberal allowance to the Company, had they not conceived themselves restrained by the principles laid down by the preceding Committee in 1805; principles however against which the Company have always protested. In consequence of this report, £1,500,000 was paid to the Company under the authority of Parliament.

In April, 1810, the Company presented to the House of Commons a supplement to their financial exposition of 1808, in which they stated the embarrassments to which they were subjected by the continued remittances of the capital of the optional India debt, and petitioned for a temporary assistance by loan. They shewed satisfactorily, that though their disposable funds were inadequate to meet the great and sudden demand on their home treasury, their property in convertible assets afforded ample security for any advance that might be made them; and on this representation Government were authorized by the act of the 50th George III. cap. 114, to issue Exchequer Bills to the amount of £1,500,000, for the use of the East India Company. By this assistance the Company's home finances were relieved for 1810. Government since that time have not only been reimbursed by the Company, in advances for the public service in India, for the above issue of Exchequer Bills, but there is a clear balance in favour of the Company (exclusive of former disputed claims), on the general account between them and Government, as made out on the 14th May, 1812, to the amount of £1,597,483, the Company taking credit on the one side for £3,630,083, expended upon the Mauritius and Java, and credit being given on the other for the sum received in Exchequer Bills.

The transfer of the debt from India to Europe having still gone on in rapid progression in the course of the last three years, and Parliament being convinced, that the operation with whatever temporary inconvenience it might be attended, would be permanently beneficial in its effects, passed an act in 1811,* authorizing the Company to make a further issue of bonds to an amount not exceeding two millions, which with the two millions issued in 1807, have produced about half a million more than the

---

* 51 George III. cap. 64.

two millions which they were empowered to add to their capital, in virtue of the act of 37th George III. cap. 3.

It being found that when the Company issue bonds to a very large amount, they are returned in payment of the goods purchased at their sales, it was deemed advisable last session of Parliament (1812), that two millions and a half should be borrowed by Government for the use of the East India Company on the same terms for which the loan was made for the public, and a clause has been introduced into the act,* binding the Company not only to provide out of their own funds for the interest of their part of the loan, but to set apart the sum of £111,820, annually, for the gradual liquidation of the principal.

In the course of the present session (1813), a further sum will still be wanted to enable the Company to meet the unprecedented demand on their home treasury, in consequence of the bills drawn upon them from India, which in the last five years, as was already stated, have amounted to the enormous sum of thirteen millions sterling. But as the utmost probable extent of these demands is now ascertained, it is to be hoped that the Company's finances (should war in India not intervene to disappoint the expectation), will be amply sufficient not only to meet the future exi-

* 52d. George III. Cap. 135.

gences of their government, but fully to discharge whatever they owe to the nation.

From the foregoing statements it appears, that the money voted to the Company by Parliament in 1805 and 1806, was in payment of an admitted debt due to them from the public. The four millions which in 1807 and 1811, the Company were empowered to raise by bonds, was in lieu of the two millions which they had the option under the 37th of the King, of adding to their capital stock. The assistance they received in 1808, was in liquidation of a debt then acknowledged to be owing to them from the public. The Exchequer bills, issued for their use in 1811, have been since repaid by advances for the public service. The only debt, therefore, which the Company now owe *to the nation* is the loan of two millions and a half borrowed in 1812; and supposing two millions and a half more to be wanted in 1813, their total debt to the public will be five millions. For the payment of the interest, and the gradual liquidation of the principal of one-half of this debt, provision has been already made, and the same provision will probably be extended to the other half when contracted. The necessity for this aid by loan might, however, have been prevented by an act of justice on the part of Government to the Company.

The unliquidated claims of the Company upon Government are,

Total estimated Excess of Disbursements on Account of His Majesty's Troops employed in India, beyond the Provisions of the Act of Parliament - - - - -	£6,200,000
Half the Expense of Ceylon and the Moluccas, and Balance on the Egyptian Expedition remaining Unpaid - - - - - - -	2,647,515
Balance in favour of the Company upon their Account with Government, as made up on the 14th May, 1812 -	1,597,483
Total Claims	£10,444,998

The payment of this debt by Government would more than enable the Company to reduce their bond debt to the sum of £1,500,000, as provided by the act of 1793, and to pay off the loan borrowed from the public in the present year, besides relieving them from the necessity of having further recourse to Parliament for assistance; and till this is done, instead of the public having ground of complaint against the Company, the Company have good reason to murmur that grievances unredressed are aggravated by unfounded accusations.

Upon the whole—In reference to *the past*, it would be unjust towards the Company, not to bear in mind that the success with which their commercial affairs have been conducted, is fully established in the reports of the select Committee of the House of Commons; that all their financial embarrassments are attributable to the political branch of the concern; and that the political measures out of which their difficulties have arisen, have been wholly adopted by the direction, and executed under the superintendence of His Majesty's Government. The politics of India, ever since the institution of the Board of Commissioners, have been considered as a branch of the general politics of the empire, and all the Company's resources, whether territorial or commercial, have been devoted to uphold the national interests to the constant injury of their trade. There has been no contrariety in the direction of measures, whatever differences of opinion may have occurred in discussion. The only apparent separation of interest has been in the settlements of accounts between the Company and the public, and in these adjustments the alacrity which the Company have at all times manifested to second the views of His Majesty's Government, as well as the uniform and brilliant success with which their operations have been accompanied, entitled their claims, at least for indemnity, to a more liberal consideration than they have sometimes met with.

With a view to *the future*, it is of essential concern to the Company,

1st.—That the number of King's troops to be maintained in India shall be definitively fixed, and that the Company shall have an indisputable claim upon His Majesty's Government for whatever expense may be incurred in consequence of any excess in their stipulated amount.

2dly.—That a principle shall be agreed upon, and regulations laid down for the adjustment of accounts between Government and the Company.

3dly.—That some mode of keeping the Company's accounts shall be devised, by which their political and commercial concerns may be preserved distinct, instead of being, as at present, inseparably interwoven.

And, 4thly.—That a system of economy be maturely concerted, and rigidly enforced upon the several Governments in India, for the purpose of checking profuse expenditure, and of retrieving the Company's finances from the embarrassments in which they are now involved.

The last of these suggestions, though obviously the most important, will not be the least difficult in the execution. There has scarcely been a single despatch sent out to India for years past, in which attention to economy has not been strongly inculcated upon the Governments abroad, and retrenchments to a considerable extent have actually been carried into effect in several branches of the service. A great clamour has been raised against the Company both here and in India, on this very account, so that they are placed in the singular predicament of having at once to encounter the obloquy attendant upon their financial embarrassments, and censure for the means they have employed, with a view to remove this subject of complaint. Private considerations, however, must give way to public expediency, and farther reforms must be projected and executed with a firmness and energy proportioned to the magnitude of the obstacles by which they are opposed. The vast extension of the Company's territories has necessarily occasioned a large increase in their establishments, both civil and military. The exhausted and dilapidated state of most of the conquered and ceded districts, requires great moderation in the demands of Government, with a view to the ultimate improvement of their resources. The internal disorders consequent upon war and rapine require vigour to repress, as well as time to heal. A display both of strength and of vigilance is necessary to overawe the lurking sentiments of jealousy and discontent, which have been powerfully excited by our success in the minds of the native Chieftains, and which are always ready to break out in acts of resistance or invasion. Those Europeans too who separate themselves from their country and connexions, and devote the best portion of their lives to dangerous and laborious duties in an unhealthy climate, have a claim to liberality on the part of their employers, which it would be equally unfeeling to overlook and senseless to disappoint. Still it must not be forgotten, that India now yields an annual revenue of more than fifteen millions and a half sterling, that the territories have been relieved from an immense load of debt, that a large saving must accrue from the reduction of the rate of interest upon the remainder, and that it is incumbent upon the local authorities to appropriate every rupee that can be spared from the necessary expenditure, to the extinction of those burdens by which the Company at home are so heavily oppressed.

In order to expose the futility of the fourth objection, viz. that the Company are bankrupts, and that they ought to share the fate of other insolvent debtors, it is only necessary to take a general view of the actual state of their affairs both abroad and at home, as exhibited in the last account of their stock, by computation, on the 1st March, 1812. A similar account is drawn up annually to the 1st March, and has been usually moved for in Parliament, as affording the most accurate and comprehensive information that could be furnished, of the state of the whole concern at the several periods when the accounts have been prepared.

Stock per Computation on the 1st of March, 1812. Dr.

To bonds bearing interest				£ 6,565,900
To ditto not bearing interest				15,417
To bills of exchange unpaid from India				4,238,382
To ditto . . . . China				43,596
To custom and excise of goods sold, and customs on goods unsold				935,318
To the Bank for a loan on mortgage of the annuities that may be sold per act of 1788				700,000
To ditto for a loan on bond				100,000
To freight and demurrage				39,336
To supra cargoes commission on all goods sold and unsold				162,800
To proprietors of private trade on all goods sold				663,000
To almshouses at Poplar				61,742
To owing for exports of former seasons				124,987
To ditto . . to the warehouse and other contingent funds				12,998
To warrants passed the Court unpaid				34,500
To owing for teas returned by the buyers and resold				971
To interest on bonds				107,891
To dividend on stock				68,932
To paid by the adventurers, being	87½ per cent. on	£3,200,000	£2,800,000	
To additional capital sold ditto	155	800,000	1,240,000	
To ditto . . . . ditto	174	1,000,000	1,740,000	
To ditto . . . . ditto	200	1,000,000	2,000,000	
		£ 6,000,000	———	7,780,000
To balance of quick stock against the Company at Bengal, made up to 30th April, 1811				17,555,313
				£ 39,211,078

The sum of £960,000, stated to be due from Government, is the balance remaining after the last payment on account of the Company's claims in the year 1808, and does not contain any disbursement on account of Government, in consequence of the late expenditure, made by the Company for expeditions from India to the Islands of Mauritius, &c. —nor does it include any extra charge incurred on account of the excess of King's troops employed in India beyond the parliamentary limit.

Stock per Computation on the 1st of March, 1812. Cr.

	£
By due from Government to the Company	1,207,560
By cash its balance on the 1st of March, 1812	995,394
By the amount of goods sold not paid for	1,096,390
By the Honourable Board of Ordnance for saltpetre	10,998
By the value of goods in England unsold	4,800,141
By balance of quick stocks in favour of the Company at Fort St. George, made up to 30th April, 1811	5,537,366
By balance of quick stocks in favour of the Company at Bombay, made up to 30th April, 1811	2,003,134
By balance of quick stocks in favour of the Company at Fort Marlborough, made up to 30th April, 1811	286,944
By balance of quick stocks in favour of the Company at Prince of Wales's Island, made up to 30th April, 1811	233,026
By balance of last books at St. Helena, made up to 30th September, 1810,	170,187
By balance of quick stocks in favour of the Company at Canton, made up to March, 1811	995,160
By balance of quick stocks in favour of the Company at the Cape of Good Hope, made up to 31st August, 1811	45,649
By cargoes from England not arrived in India and China, at the dates of the several quick stocks	1,876,872
By exports paid for, exclusive of bullion season, 1811-12	1,283,926
By impress and war allowances paid owners of ships not arrived in England	665,043
By the value of ships, sloops, and vessels, exclusive of those stationed abroad	70,020
By the value of East India House and warehouses	1,138,000
By the Company paid for their dead stock in India	400,000
By due from Government for stores and supplies to His Majesty's troops	960,000
By ditto on account of hemp from India	120,801
By owing from sundry persons returned from India and in India, to be repaid in England	19,712
	23,922,013
Balance against	15,289,065
	£ 39,211,078

MEMORANDUM:—

In the above account the article of dead stock is valued at £400,000, which includes buildings and fortifications, plate, household furniture, plantations, farms, sloops, vessels, stores, and other articles of dead stock, according to Lord Godolphin's award in the year 1702, whereas the whole of the sums of money expended in buildings and fortifications, by the last advices from the Company's several settlements, for the acquisition and maintenance of their possessions, and the nearest estimated value of other articles of dead stock, is as follows:

	Buildings and Fortifications.	Plate, Household Furniture, Plantations, Farms, Sloops, Vessels, Stores, &c.	TOTAL.
At Bengal	£ 5,079,150	£ 1,483,015	£ 6,562,165
— Fort St. George & sub.	1,887,313	464,209	2,351,522
— Bombay and ditto	1,102,586	345,690	1,448,276
— Fort Marlborough	244,810	66,889	311,699
— St. Helena	43,856	98,905	142,761
	£ 8,357,715	£ 2,458,708	£ 10,816,423

The balance against the Company by the foregoing account is £15,289,065. This balance, however, is more apparent than real, as will be manifest from the following observations.

In the first place, on the debtor side of the account, is included (contrary to usual custom) the capital advanced by the proprietors, amounting to £7,780,000. This cannot properly be considered as a debt, because it has not created a liability of demand. Its extinction (supposing it to be extinguished) can only be esteemed a loss sustained by the subscribers—a misfortune from which they alone are the sufferers. Deducting therefore the sum of £7,780,000 subscribed by the adventurers, from the unfavourable balance as above stated, that balance will be reduced to £7,509,065.

2. Credit is only taken for £400,000, on account of what has been paid for dead stock in India, amounting, as per memorandum, to £10,816,423. As a considerable part of the latter sum must have been laid out on perishable articles, many of which are greatly deteriorated, and some not now in existence, it would be extravagant to claim credit for the whole amount of the expenditure. It is obvious, however, that the valuation put upon the property denominated Dead Stock in 1702, can bear but a very small proportion to its actual value, and the subsequent increase (whatever it is) ought to be set down in deduc-

tion of the unfavourable balance against the Company on the general account.

3. Credit is only taken for sums due from Government to the Company to the amount (as per 1st and 19th items of the account) of £2,167,560, whereas it has been already shewn, that the sum actually due, or at least for which the Company have a fair claim to reimbursement, amounted on the 14th May, 1812, to £10,444,998.

4. Whatever difference of opinion may exist as to the Company's right to the sovereignty of those territories which have been acquired in India by conquest and treaties, nothing is more just than that not only the territorial debt as it now stands should accompany the territorial sovereignty, but that whatever sum the territory has borrowed from the trade, should be repaid in the event of a separation of interests. The balance of clear profit in favour of the Company's Commerce, is reported by the Select Committee of the House of Commons to have amounted between 1793-4 to 1809-10, to £2,164,533, which sum has been expended in supplies to the political concern, and were the two branches of the concern henceforth to be conducted under different auspices, a final adjustment of accounts must take place between them, in which case the sum above stated would constitute a claim on the part of the trade against the territory. The Company would also

have a claim upon Government for the losses they have sustained by supplies of hemp, and by the excess of saltpetre furnished to the Board of Ordnance, beyond the quantity stipulated in the original agreement.

5. The only privilege now enjoyed by the Company, which is determinable at the expiration of their Charter, is that of carrying on the *exclusive* trade to and from India and China, and other places beyond the Cape of Good Hope. Supposing the renewal of this privilege to be refused, the Company cannot be bereaved of their perpetual right, as a body corporate, to trade with India and China upon a joint stock, in common with the rest of their fellow subjects. Supposing, also, that the territories which have been acquired in India by conquest and treaty, with the debt contracted in their acquisition, were assumed by the Crown, the Company have large estates in India, their titles to which are as indefeisible as any that money can purchase, or the most legitimate occupancy has ever established, and which could not therefore be legally comprehended in this assumption. Of this description are the town of Calcutta and the twenty-four Purgunnahs—Madras and its Jaghire—the five northern Circars—the islands of Bombay and St. Helena—Cuddalore, Penang, and Bencoolen, and all the forts and factories held by the Company under original grants from the native Princes in India. Of these possessions the Company

cannot be deprived without an equivalent compensation, unless the British Parliament, forsaking the common principles of justice, shall choose by an arbitrary proceeding to invade the rights of property, which have uniformly been respected in its past decisions. The estates, as enumerated, ought therefore to be admitted in the schedule of the Company's disposable assets.

6. When it is considered that the whole unfavourable balance against the Company upon the general account (including their capital stock) falls short of one year's revenue of their Indian territories, the state of the concern instead of being desperate, may be held forth with exultation as exhibiting an instance of successful enterprise unparalleled either in ancient or modern times.

To those who are not disposed to acknowledge the extension, internal improvement, and additional security of the Indian empire, to be a sufficient compensation for the sacrifices by which these objects have been attained, the following extract from the conclusion of the fourth report of the Select Committee of the House of Commons, will present a different and perhaps more consolatory view of the subject.*

* 4th Report, pages 454, 455.

"Your Committee having referred in their third "report to considerations that seemed, in their "judgment, to offer some counterbalance to the "sacrifices of funds which had been made, conceive "it unnecessary to introduce any additional remarks "on this head; but after calling to the recollection "of the House, that the observations hitherto made "on these extensive and complicated transac-"tions, and on the result of them, have applied "exclusively to the interests of the East India "Company, your Committee will proceed to submit "their view of them in their bearing on the general "interests of the British Empire, which they trust is "such as to lead to results much more gratifying "than those which have been exhibited in reference "to the separate affairs of the Company. The in-"voice value of goods and stores exported by "the East India Company to India, China, "and St. Helena, between 1791-2 and 1807-8 was "£29,244,227; deducting the amount lost and cap-"tured, £28,791,967. There was exported in bul-"lion in the same period £9,434,042. The total "export from England, supposed to have arrived "between 1792-3 and 1808-9, was, therefore, "£38,226,009. The returns made by India and "China in consignments of goods amounted to "£50,754,400. The charges upon these goods, "not added to the invoices, may be stated at "£2,916,279, which will carry the amount of the "returns to the sum of £53,670,679, exclusive of

" £1,371,788 lost and captured. On which view " it will appear that England received in property " from India and China, more than was sent, to the " amount of £15,444,670; but the result arising out " of the transactions of the East India Company " alone is susceptible of a very considerable addition, " if the means existed of examining with equal accu- " racy the exports and imports in privilege and " private trade. The amount of the exports it is not " practicable at all to ascertain; neither can the " value of the imports be shewn, otherwise than by " a general computation governed by the proportion " between the prime cost and the sale amount of the " Company's goods. The sale amount of the privi- " lege and private trade and neutral property was " £37,794,857, the prime cost of which may be " calculated at £20,700,000. How far the pur- " chase of these goods was made by exports from " England, it is not possible to state; but no doubt " exists of the purchase of them in this manner hav- " ing been very considerably below the amount of " the prime cost now stated. Whatever the amount " of the exports may have been, the difference be- " tween that and the sum of £20,700,000 is so " much in addition to the result above shewn, which " would be still further enhanced by the remittance " of fortunes known to have been made in a variety " of shapes, from India to England, through extra- " neous and circuitous channels, to an amount

" which there is no possibility of tracing with accu-" racy.

" If the means were attainable of shewing the " result upon accurate calculations, the advantages " derived to the British Empire would appear to a " very large amount. The same difficulty, however, " does not obstruct a statement of the accession " accruing to the general circulation, and the bene-" fits derived from it both to India and England. In " India the industry of the subject has been encou-" raged and assisted by the employment of forty-" six millions sterling, or on the annual average " £2,700,000 in the provision of investments for " England.

" The produce and manufactures of India pur-" chased by this sum, combined with those of China " sold in England, realized in sale amount to the " extent of nearly one hundred and forty-one mil-" lions sterling, or more than eight millions per " annum. The general distribution and circulation " arising out of this trade may be stated to have " been,

" In the purchase of the produce and ma-" nufactures of England	£29,200,000
" In the employment of British shipping	25,000,000
" In the payment of bills of exchange	24,500,000

	£
" In the purchase of bullion, the import " of which may be supposed to have " been in payment for British produce	9,400,000
" In disbursements for home charges .	11,600,000
" In dividends to proprietors of capital " stock and interest in bonds . .	12,500.000

" The sale of private goods and neutral property " amounted to nearly £37,800,000. Of this sum " about four millions may be supposed to be in- " cluded above. If an adjustment could be made of " the remainder, amounting to £33,800,000, the " distribution of it could be precisely defined.

" It has appeared that the duties on imports, col- " lected through the Company, and realized at a " very trivial expense to Government, amounted to " £39,300,000, and on exports to £660,000; toge- " ther £39,960,000.

" The combination of these several sums, producing " £185,960,000, shews, that on the average of the " last seventeen years, £10,900,000 per annum has " been diffused in various channels through the whole " circulation of the British empire. By this its " manufactures have been supported, encouraged, " and improved; its shipping has been increased, " its revenues augmented, its commerce extended,

" its agriculture promoted, and its power and re-" sources invigorated and upheld."

Such are the advantages which the new Parliament will be solicited by the East India Company to secure to the Country, under a continuance of the existing system, and which it will be importuned by other classes to hazard in favour of one of the wildest schemes that ever entered into the head of man, through " the ivory gate of dreams." Sir Francis Bacon has well observed, " It is not good to try " experiments in States, except the necessity be " urgent, or the utility be evident; and well to " beware that it be reformation that draweth on the " change, and not the desire of change that pretend-" eth the reformation; and, lastly, that the novelty, " though it be not rejected, yet be held for suspect, " and as the scripture saith—*That we make a stand* " *upon the ancient way, and then look about us, and* " *discover what is the straight and right way, and so to* " *walk in it.*"*

" The science of constructing a Commonwealth," says another illustrious author, " or renovating it, " or reforming it, is like every other experimental " science, not to be taught *a priori;* nor is it a short " experience that can instruct in that practical

* Essay on Innovation.

" science, because the real effects of moral causes " are not always immediate, but that which in the " first instance is prejudicial, may be excellent in " its remoter operation; and its excellence may arise " even from the ill effects it produces in the beginning. The reverse also happens; and plausible " schemes with very pleasing commencements have " often shameful and lamentable conclusions. In " States there are some obscure and almost latent " causes, things which appear at first view of little " moment, on which a very great part of their " prosperity or adversity may most essentially depend. The science of Government, therefore, " being so practical in itself, and intended for such " practical purposes, a matter which requires experience, and even more experience than any person " can gain in his whole life, however sagacious and " observing he may be, it is with infinite caution " that any man ought to venture upon pulling down " an edifice which has answered in any tolerable " degree for ages the practical purposes of society, " or upon building it up again without having models and patterns of approved utility before his " eyes."*

The East India Company has answered in an eminent degree the ends of its establishment, and what-

* Burke's Reflections.

ever may be the theoretical objections to which its constitution is liable, it has contributed more to the wealth, prosperity, and power of Great Britain, and done more to advance her fame in the opinion of the world, than ever was achieved by any even of her most favourite institutions. It is to be hoped that it is not destined by its fall to perpetuate the ingratitude, rashness, and folly of the times, without even gracing the Country with a noble ruin. Like the celebrated statue which, so long as it adorned the harbour of Rhodes, was accounted one of the wonders of the world, but which, when broken down, served only to load twelve hundred asses with fragments of old brass, the Colossus of the Company is magnificent in form, and imposing in dimensions, but if demolished, its disjointed materials will be found of little value to those whose efforts are now directed to its overthrow.

FINIS.